CONCRETE APPROXIMATIONS —

CONCRETE APPROXIMATIONS — In Pursuit of Absolute Space

OLIVIER OTTEVAERE

APPLIED
RESEARCH
AND
DESIGN
PUBLISHING

Typset in
Novato, CA

CONTENTS

CONCRETE APPROXIMATIONS

A thing of the Past

My obsession with concrete began as a third-year student at the Cooper Union. Broadly speaking the curriculum was shaped around the recurring idea of 'design as analysis' and 'analysis as design'. While studying, we were encouraged to materialise design questions and hypotheses in the workshop. The intent was to construct and hone our own architectural language by the end of thesis, first as a form of resistance to joining the mainstream profession, second as a provision to kick off an independent career, in the same way that, for example Daniel Libeskind or Elizabeth Diller began their careers. The free education model was also there for students to emulate the live architecture endeavor and autonomous work of some of the key figures who taught during my education there: J. Hejduk ('builder of worlds'), R. Abraham ('Un-Built'), P. Eisenman ('Houses of cards'), R. Scofidio ('Flesh'), L. Woods ('Radical re-construction'), D. Agrest ('Oppositions') and so on. Some, self-proclaimed 'last visionaries' had strong yet contrasting ideologies towards architecture, backed up by unique, substantial and progressive bodies of work, somewhat uncompromising and autonomous. They influenced my thinking in conceptualising projects, in a search for a new over-arching architectural language, that is part of a work in series, that make use of a process-based method of design, exploring and testing ideas through iterations, transformations of precedents and geometrical and physical operations.

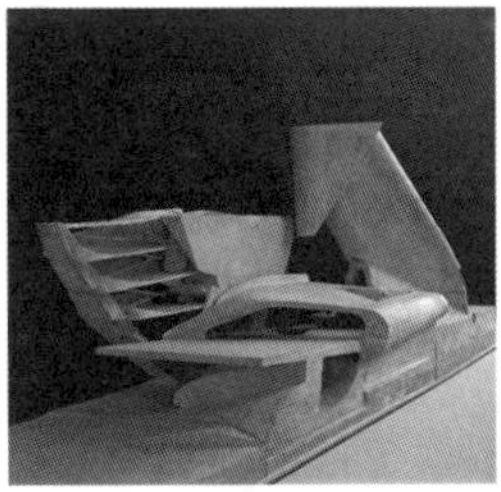

Fig. 1: Concrete cast model (two meters long, made in three parts with ground), Newtown Creek: Urban Farm, from hand-crafted geometrical drawings to analogue methods of making in the workshop (pre-digital fabrication), by O. Ottevaere and A. Rochas, Year 3 project, the Cooper Union, 2000.

Design through Prototyping

So why concrete? At the time, the choice was largely intuitive. It was felt that there were more opportunities, in working with the material, for exploration or experimentation than were offered by other material processes. Dealing with concrete is multi-step and non-linear. Its material properties are greatly active, i.e., fluid pressure, yet temporal, with the progression through its states practically irreversible, e.g., liquid to solid mass. The non-deterministic take on 'design through prototyping' is what constitutes the main line of inquiry. Discoveries arise from an open process informed by the interactions of materials via their physical properties. More specifically, some materials need to give room to others in order to perform in less predictable ways within a process of making. This indirect approach to design is probably exacerbated by the adoption of concrete as the favored material of use in most of the key projects. It is a material with which one can still approximate while having to retain precise measures. Fluctuating between approximate precision and concrete approximation is a main attitude towards design as contribution to a methodology primarily built on material prototyping.

Concrete Culture

Concrete is culturally contentious. The architecture it produces, however, remains pertinent to history and not least, it has retained its relevance across fields and practices to this day. It is also environmentally controversial, although it can be either beneficial or harmful, depending which side of the coin you argue for[1], e.g., the way in which cement is industrially produced (carbon intensive) versus how concrete is used in building construction (thermal mass that can increase thermal comfort). Having been normalised, misused and abused over decades by different stakeholders and for various reasons and agendas, its material attributes remain very much untapped. In fact, it is full of endless possibilities when approached from its mould; the formwork or falsework, as it is technically referred to in the building industry.

Concrete Formwork

Making falseworks, the moulding into which concrete will be poured, demonstrates the real potential in challenging what concrete can do. It requires the need to place much attention and resources on a temporary, but the most crucial part of a project, that will eventually disappear. If it was not for the traces of forces once at stake, left behind, it would have been hard to imagine that it even existed, as its technical name suggests. Devising falsework gives the designer a form of productive resistance about the work to come, one where the properties of the material, e.g., pressure, fluidity, continuity, mass and weight could briefly be let free, tweaked and once again be re-invigorated. The indirectness involved in prototyping formwork is what can give concrete its uniqueness in comparison to other materials' one-step processes. Procedurally, a sense of productive material uncertainty is left open for new discoveries.

Concrete Fluidity

When considered as a process, concrete in essence is just a liquid mass inside a short-lived space: the formwork itself. The prototyping part of the projects takes priority, in gambling as much as possible on that brief moment of fluidity, with the aim to extend the fluid stone past its solid state and in doing so, registering its frozen forces. The idea of mass or massing, solid-void relations, light and heavy in the work is also informed by engaging directly with the material per se and its unique properties.

To enable fluidity, a relative degree of responsiveness needs to take place between the formwork materials and the concrete properties. This balancing act, in letting materials compute and negotiate their ultimate formations, appears at first approximate, as the initial formwork setup is relatively uncertain. Only through an iterative process, supported by clearly defined geometries, can one begin to control their precise calibration and ultimate fine-tuning. The idea of material responsiveness is only one active part of this notion of uncertainty. Another facet of uncertainty is in the spatial and temporal interaction of concrete formations, with its immediate environment through the medium of light. This phenomenon is first unfolded in Chapter 1, through the New Order project and then further assessed in Chapter 2 with Casa Trevo.

1 Forty, A. 2012. Concrete and Culture, a Material History: pp. 69-78 Reaktion Books LTD, London.

Overall, the projects strive to elevate concrete as a material by manipulating its properties and by prototyping formworks. Chapter 1 begins that exploration on fluidity and continuity through a series of concrete cast column experiments named New Orders where a set of techniques, part of a toolbox developed through the project, is presented as an attempt to demonstrate what can unfold from an approach to prototyping, its speculative nature, its relevance to architectural design and also where some of its limitations may lie.

TOOLBOX OF TECHNIQUES AND GRAMMAR SHAPING: NEW ORDERS

Fig. 1: Display of seven columns of New Orders, Hong Kong, China, 2016.

Through the lens of a specific project, New Orders, nine concrete columns of 1.8 meters high, was created using a toolbox of techniques. The techniques are a result of experimenting with various systems of formworks for concrete casting and with analogue methods of form findings. They also investigate the potential for the resulting concrete casts to project new spatial arrangements, helping to shape a particular architecture grammar for future architecture works.

This toolbox continues to evolve from project to project and in scale. In fact, some of the columns' formal and spatial outcomes were instrumental in shaping the early design strategy and programmatic organisation of the house Casa Trevo, explained later. Presented below is a selection of these techniques and associated issues, such as the value of prototyping, the role of an iterative process, the use of precedent studies, the potential of inhabiting scales, the ways of making and the benefits of mixing methods in a design process.

New Orders is an independent project that was self-initiated as a practice-research endeavor. The outcome of the small-scale experiments is nine concrete cast columns. It proposes a singular work, made in a series where one column leads to another from an open-ended process of making.

The project remains an important resource in the early design of new projects and in directing new research paths. From a material standpoint, the concrete columns are experiments in fluidity, searching for better transitions between tectonic elements as well as for new forms of continuity enabled by the liquid material.

In general, the columns are investigated at two scales: At scale of 1:1, as columns, they open up a direct process of prototyping with the concrete

Fig.2: New Orders: nine concrete cast columns (approx. 180cm high by 35cm wide) made in Hong Kong, China, 2014-2016.

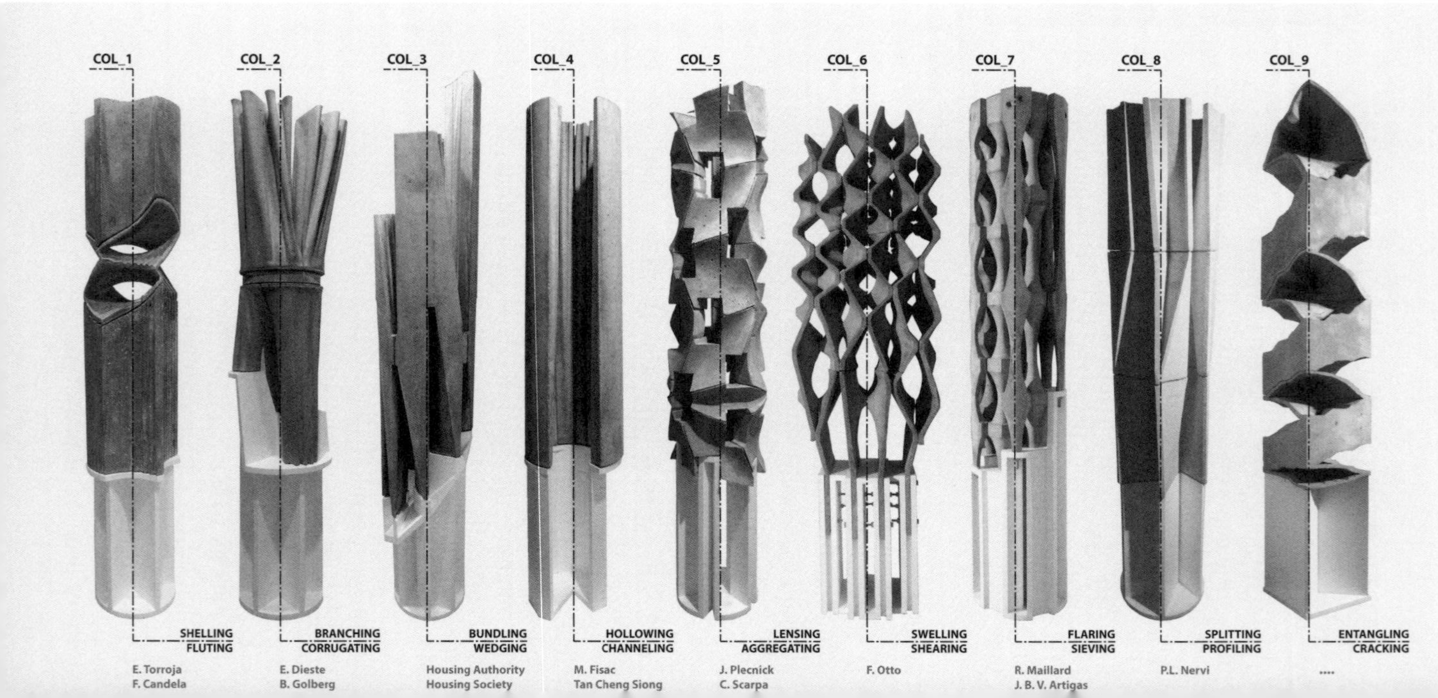

material, exploring numerous formwork methods in incremental ways to provide a formal grammar and a toolbox of making techniques. At scale of 1:100, as towers, they are speculative of spatial organisations for vertical living relating to Hong Kong, China and serve as a first reading of the possibilities given by the massing of the columns. That side of the work was mainly conducted through analytical drawings and diagramming.

Precedent Studies

The project's point of contention and critique lies in the universal cast-in-place concrete frame. The modernist search for new concrete-based models for living, fuelled by an urgent need for cheap housing after the destruction of the Second World War, was devised in Western Europe in the form of a cast-in-place skeleton frame. In the late 19th century, this flexible column-slab system was first patented and distributed by the Francois Hennebique's business, supported globally by licensed agents and concessionary contractors[2]. Hennebique's focus on reinforced concrete structures prompted the initial schism between architectural design and technical construction.

Antis

In 1914, Le Corbusier generalised a two-storey column slab structure, known as the Domino protocol; a portmanteau for domus and innovation. Its promise was social; to support individualisation of living spaces by internally liberating the plan of a building from its structural imperatives; the Free Plan. This mass-produced and standardised construction method provided its future inhabitants with a plain and low-cost framework to be individualised based on means, aspirations and identity. What the Dom-ino model essentially offered, by highlighting the slab, was the idea of an empty plan; new ground, released from the literal one[3]. This quickly projected the possibility of envisioning a multiplicity of 'free' grounds, as slabs, and whose sequence of spatial organisations would not need to be identical anymore. The concept of

2 Gubler, J. 1993. *Les Beautes du Beton Armee. Le Beton en representation. La Memoire Photographique de L'entreprise Hennebique 1890-1930*: pp. 13-24. Editions Hazan, Paris.

Fig. 3-5: The 'Structural Mavericks' versus 'Maison Dom-ino' (1914) by Le Corbusier and the generic concrete frame.

3 Aureli, P. V. 2014. The Dom-ino Problem: Questioning the Architecture of Domestic Space. In C. Davidson (ed.) *Log* 30: pp. 160-168. Anyone Corporation, New York.

repetition of differences vs. sameness has struggled to this day to fulfill its early assignment. On the contrary, the structural ideal largely continues to overshadow its architectural benefits, caused by a preoccupation for high efficiency, great economy of means and for the minimal labour skills it demands. A century later, this now ubiquitous structural system has largely achieved the reverse: mainly creating an order characterised by homogeneity based on the repetition of the same living units across many building scales.

However, the advent of structural reinforced concrete originated long before Le Corbusier's 1914 icon. Much of the required experimentation had taken place over half a century prior to any practical and theoretical formulations. Architects and engineers were not the biggest advocates for the potential of this new hybrid in concrete and steel and continuous material. Many of the physical undertakings, conducted around 1850, through successive trial and error efforts at full scale, were carried out by builders and contractors, i.e., J. Monier, F. Coignet or J. Lambot in their own back gardens[4].

If one considers concrete as process, and not just concrete as material, what has just been introduced above, might not appear so modern, after all. Like the timber structures previously used in construction, these 'new' reinforced concrete systems do not capitalise enough on the properties of the material; a liquid and continuous agent. For the most part, they have more efficiently repeated existing structural systems using a new material. Instead of being restricted to an amalgam of predefined rigid elements (post, beam and slab, more suitable for timber and steel), greater design investments in formwork methods might contribute greatly to the quest for new volumetric continuity and for different spatial organisations, beyond efficiency and practicality. In this respect, technology and innovation must be less concerned with the material's imperatives per se, but rather strive to emulate the range of discoveries that emerged from the early empirical methods in concrete constructions.

4 Forty, A. 2012. *Concrete and Culture, a Material History*: pp. 16-20. Reaktion Books LTD, London.

Pros

It was only after the Second World War that non-conformists came to reconsider the full potential that reinforced concrete had suggested at its origin. Sometimes called the structural rationalists, personalities like Eduardo Torroja, Pier Luigi Nervi, Felix Candela, Heinz Isler, and Robert Maillart, pushed to great effects the true premises of the original material: a short-lived liquid mass in space, in search of new solid formations.

To address this, they placed a strong emphasis on experimentation towards the development of formwork design, supported by well-articulated geometries and methods of construction that would liberate concrete once again from an all too safe and predicable approach.

But the restored attitude towards structural concrete did not come without a high level of risk taking and occasional failures. These structural mavericks took reinforced concrete to the limit of what the new material could do, both structurally and spatially. New Orders pays homage to their ambitious work and inspiration and also uses their process as a good practice methodology for experimentation.

Transformations

Column 1 draws from the history of thin shell structures, specifically by revisiting Felix Candela's work on Hyperbolic Paraboloid, also known as Hypar. Warped surfaces, efficiently described by a series of rotating lines—e.g., ruled geometry—and in close proximity with its resulting formwork procedure, serve as the principal spatial and structural element for the void description at the column's centre[5]. It proposes a sequence of semi-public outdoor spaces created within the shaft of a column through perforations, while aiming for a high degree of structural integrity. Instead of considering saddle structures as single storey, like in the work of Candela, the prototype instigates their potential to stack up into a

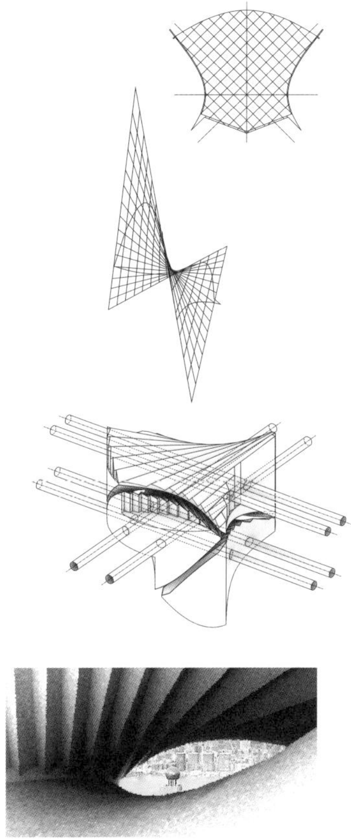

Fig. 6-8: Column 1: diagrams of F. Candela's hypar described by ruled geometry / its transformation to formwork prototype of the column's mid-section / its habitation as public space inside tower.

5 Garlock M.E.M. & Billington D.P. 2008. *Discipline of the Hyperbolic Paraboloid. Felix Candela, Engineer, Builder, Structural Artist*: pp. 76-87. Yale University Press, New Haven.

vertical compound of interchanging vaults. Four rotating hypars of varied amplitudes interlock to describe three successive occupiable voids within a vertical shaft.

Column 6 makes use of Frei Otto's high and low points' tensile membranes. The simplicity of Frei Otto's original geometry, economically described by a set of high and low points[6] is transposed vertically to create a sequence of interconnected shear walls. A constellation of positive and negative vectors to the original planes of the walls distorts them to form bulges that bind the walls together. This set of protuberances not only provides greater lateral resistance to the wall structure but also contains varied spaces prompting the principal organisation of the living units for the project; it is receptive to light, front and back, and to air transversally.

Column 7 starts with Robert Maillart's beamless mushroom slab structure. He proposed to flare the top of his columns to decrease the bending points in the slab, usually resisted by a set of beams. Not only did Maillart's columns flare upwards to distribute the ceiling loads across larger areas, but in other projects they also flared downwards to reduce pressure on the soil foundation. The elimination of beams allowed the slab and columns to perform as a monolith connection[7]. The column prototype takes advantage of the doubly-flared primitive, e.g., at top and bottom, vertically repeating it to create a compound of 13 tall and slender elements of various periodicities and of changing density in section. The primary aim is to reorganise a multi-storey high-rise into partial aggregations of horizontal instances, unevenly distributed across the height of a column, which as a result breaks the dominance of the horizontal slab and blurs the line between interior and exterior spaces.

Column 8 begins with the study of Pier Luigi Nervi's columns of varying sections found in much of his built work.

6 Glaeser, L. 1972. *The Work of Frei Otto*: pp. 105-122. The Museum of Modern Art, New York.

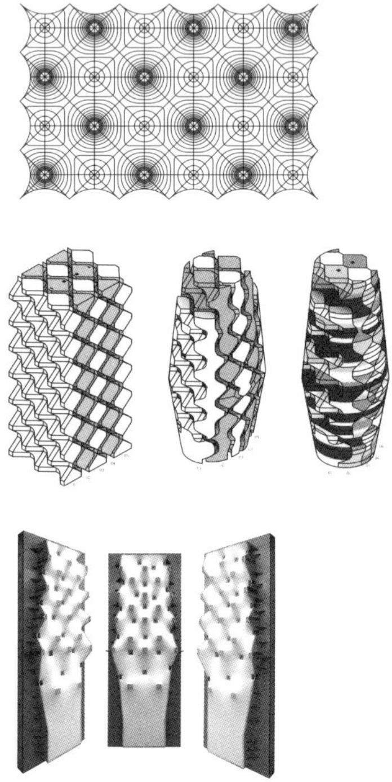

Fig. 9-11: Column 6: Plan diagram of F. Otto's high and low points' tensile membrane / its transformation to column massing / its translation to formwork prototype.

7 Mivelaz, P. 2008. Mushroom Head, Pilzdecke, pilier-champignon: metamorphoses de la dalle sans sommiers. In R. Gargiani (ed.) *La Colonne, Nouvelle Histoire de la Construction*: pp. 237-51. Presses polytechniques and universitaires romandes, Lausanne.

8 Nervi, P. L. 1965. *Aesthetics and Technology in Building: The Plastic Richness of Concrete Cast in Place*: pp. 23-36. Harvard University Press, Cambridge, Massachusetts.

Due to its plastic properties, reinforced concrete permitted Nervi to transform a column's profile from top to bottom in order to respond to different structural demands. Informed by objective static and construction considerations, the transition from changing sections is negotiated by straight lines connecting points on the contours of each section[8]. The column prototype appropriates this geometrical procedure in vertical deformation.

First, various two-dimensional sections are identified within the height of the column. Next, their differences are geometrically interpolated by a series of rotating straight lines to generate a range of recessed spaces, carving out the mass of the column more and more towards its top.

The examples above convey how the column prototypes depart from an understanding of precedent studies in order to draw new design hypotheses for the columns' series. A prototyping process then triggers the precedents' radical transformations as a means to condition new material and spatial organisations for the concrete columns. Although one could detect formal traces from some of the precedents used in the finish work, the columns do not refer back to them to legitimise the existence of their massing. An important precept for the project was that ultimately the columns became autonomous; precedents were not used to make a historical or theoretical critique of the project. Rather, they were left as inspirational points of departure only.

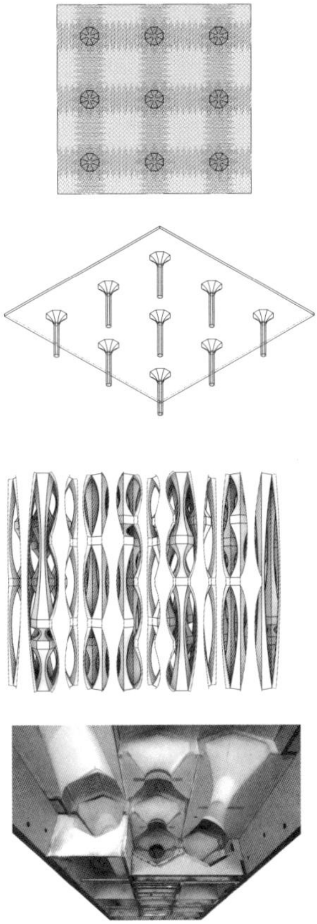

Fig. 12-14: Column 7: Bottom view diagram of Robert Maillart's mushroom slab / unfolded elevation of its transformation into column / its translation to formwork prototype.

The Value of Prototyping

A differentiation needs to be made between prototyping and prototype in research-practice. The original meaning of 'to prototype' is 'to first strike' at something ('protos': first, 'tupos': to strike), which differs slightly from a prototype, which is described as a 'typical form of something; an archetype'. A prototype is an outcome, a product of some sort that one can arrive at from multiple ways, e.g., from other types of processes than prototyping. It is often confused with something that is generic or universal enough to become highly adaptable to many external factors. The 'Maison Dom-ino' by Le Corbusier would best fit that description.

Alternatively, prototyping is an endeavour; a process of iterations where one is directly engaged with searching for something else that at best cannot be premeditated. What that something else might be is less relevant and might always remain speculative and far ahead of the process itself. Instead, what matters are the potential discoveries made along the way that hold the possibility of defining new design-research trajectories, beyond process for process's sake. That is the reason why working with concrete can be so productive. Implicitly tackling the material requires procedures that are non-linear but multi-stepped. Concrete as material per se is the end result of that process of experimentation, the moment of solid verification. Whereas when one considers concrete as process, it all becomes about what has come before, in prototyping formworks with a range of other materials and properties.

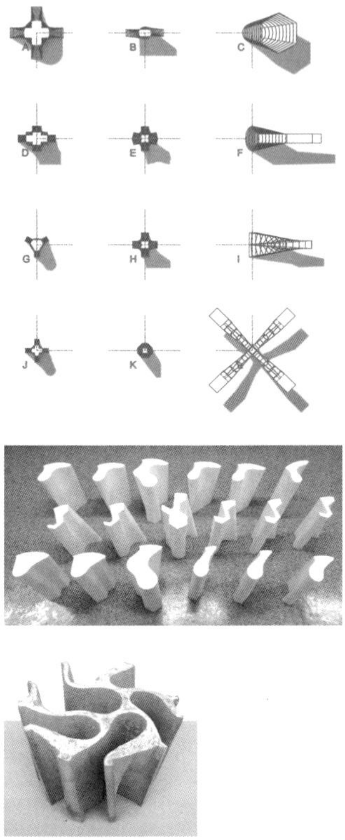

Fig. 15-17: Column 8: Plan diagram of P. L. Nervi's columns of changing profiles / transformation to a series of formwork pieces mediating changes in profile from top to bottom / first iteration of concrete test.

Mixing Methods

Column_2 presents a specific way of working, demonstrating how various design methods and strategies interchange. Each one informs others in turn, meaning the roles they play in the prototyping development of the project are further revealed. Iterations and transformations of these techniques across multiple columns are discussed later in the chapter. Such aspects, discussed below, are the use of geometry, the transformation of precedents, the development of formwork, the effects from materials, the translation to inhabitation, and concepts of ground.

Fig. 18: Final assembly of parts of concrete column_3 onto wooden base, showing the column's relation to human scale.

Aim

What the primary massing set out to do for this design was to create a branching and ribbon-like column at 1:1 scale. The column's central bulk is

Fig. 19: Column_2 prototype under different lighting conditions; morning, noon and afternoon.

able to split into smaller footprints: downwards to engage with an irregular stepped ground surface; and upwards to maximise light penetration and air circulation to living units, as well as influencing their spatial and programmatic organisations. Additionally, to increase the structural performance of the splitting column, a corrugated wall is introduced that also performs as a delineator of space between inside and outside living at 1:100 scale. The formal variation in plan across the height of the column shaft accounts for the further diversity of living types.

Relational Geometry

A distinction needs to be made in the work between form, geometry and figure. Of course, one cannot deny that the final columns of New Orders have a relatively pronounced yet diverse formal appearance. However, they are not formally driven in the sense that an overall form is predefined and dictates the project's evolution. Instead, a set of geometric relationships are established early in the columns' development based on the design intents. Their weighting is constantly re-evaluated at each step of the process in support of design operations and transformations. In the case of column_2, it begins with a simple primitive that captures the main design concept at 1:1 scale; the splitting column as shown in the drawing sequence on the right. Complexity then progressively builds up, all the way to its speculative inhabitation at scale 1:100. In parallel, formwork prototypes are developed incrementally, e.g., from simple to more elaborate, to provide feedback on the overall development of the column and tower concurrently.

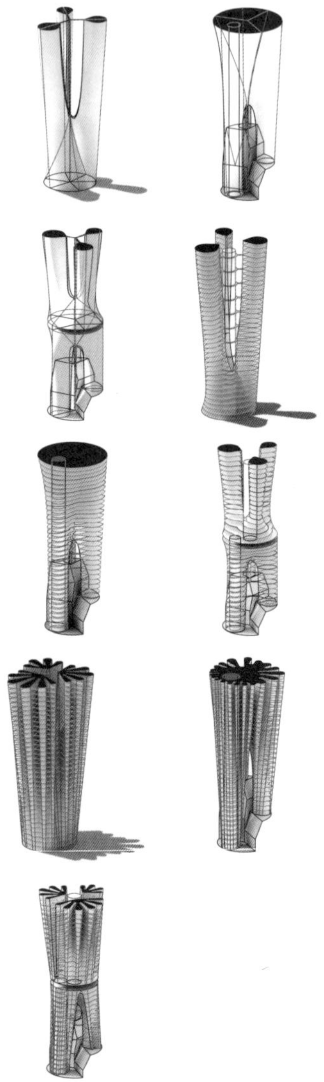

Fig. 20-28: Geometrical progression from primitive massing (1:1) to spatial organisation for living (1:100).

The geometrical figures in the columns and in the work in general, are often rounded or curvilinear and never solely planar with sharp edges. The reason is concrete. Internally, it is to liberate the fluid and continuous reading the concrete material permits. Externally, it is to render a particular effect of light; one that is zonal, whose light-to-shadow boundaries are blurred or a

Fig. 29-30: Plan geometry of splitting column mass and its first massing translation to formwork.

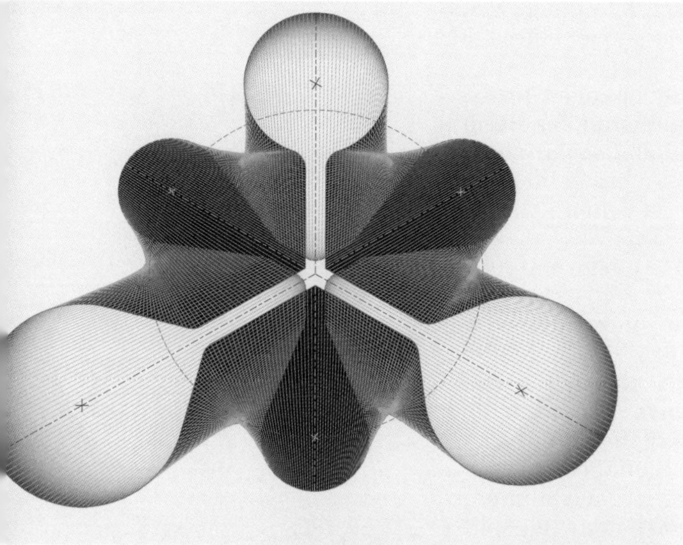

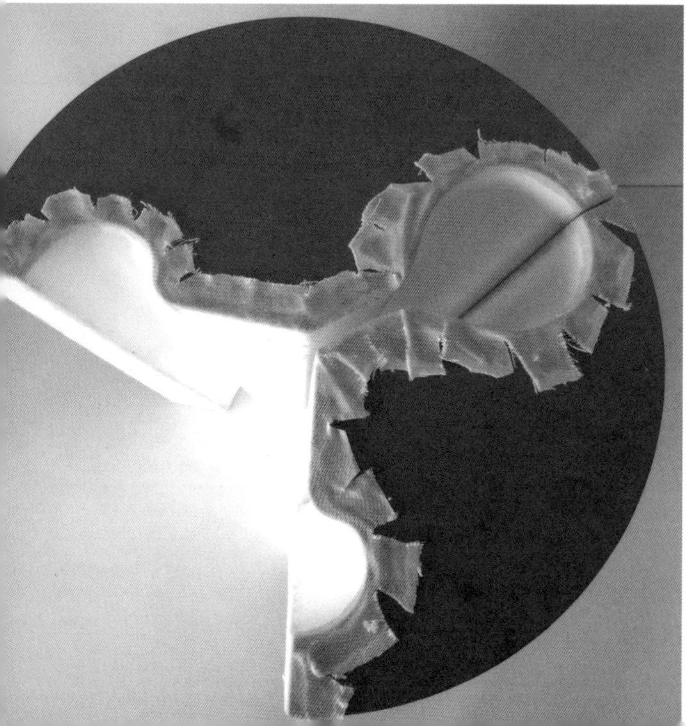

gradient. In doing so, the columns not only retain their volumetric reading but the play of light and shadow on their surfaces accentuates their mass perception at different levels of detail, e.g., from global to local. In addition, geometric figures, like the circle, are used as visual references in the built work to demarcate formal changes, transforming from a primitive or a default condition to other material, formal, spatial and scalar characteristics, e.g., the branching of a circle into three smaller undulating footprints in column_2.

Precedents Extractions & Transformations

Column_2 was initiated by the study of Pier Luigi Nervi's columns of changing profiles, by Eladio Dieste's vertical ruled surfaces, and by Bertrand Goldberg's ribbon wall buildings. The branching out idea for the overall massing of column_2 was inspired by Nervi's transitional columns, conceived to address different structural imperatives at top and bottom, in particular the split columns that were used for the Italian embassy in Brasilia (1969). Eladio's use of conoids to amplify the surface of a wall[9], as in his church of 'Christ the Worker' (Atlantida, Uruguay, 1960), not only informed the augmented structural resistance to the overhanging arms of the column, but also determined its spatial and living organisation. Goldberg's 'River City I' project (1979, unbuilt) more explicitly supported the evolution of the typical plan for the column inhabitation at scale 1:100. It did so by revisiting the effectiveness of its ribbon wall, delineating the tower's internal housing program. Its influence on the column's organisation is further discussed below in 'Column Inhabitation'.

Formwork Prototyping

The column's formwork strategy makes use of one of the techniques I called 'Analogue Computation' explained later in greater detail in 'Ways of Making'. In brief, the best way to interpolate a complex surface mediating from an arc profile at one end to a corrugated curve at the other was by

Fig. 31-33: Diagrammatic studies of Eladio Dieste's conoids / Pier Luigi Nervi's columns of changing profiles / Bertrand Goldberg's ribbon wall.

9 Ochsendorf, J. A. 2004. *Eladio Dieste as Structural Artist. Eladio Dieste, Innovation in Structural Art*: pp. 94-96. Princeton Architectural Press, New York.

letting a stretched sheet of fabric compute the intermediary three-dimensional geometry, almost freely.

Not only does the textile generate an optimal surface, it also exudes a relative amount of tensile force, captured in the formwork itself and later imprinted in the concrete cast; this is an intentional and important characteristic in the concrete projects in general, described later in 'Material Accentuations'. This refinement to the formwork technique demanded several iterations to master, constituting a part of the overall prototyping endeavour. The profiles themselves, used to make the timber frame of the formwork, are not arbitrary shapes but geometrically correspond to the plans developed in parallel at scale 1:100. As the column design matures, both active scales become increasingly synchronised.

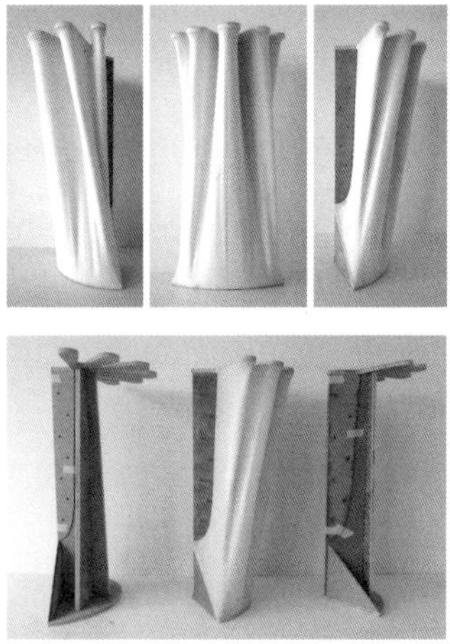

Fig. 34-35: Second negative formwork iteration with integration of corrugations as spatial delineator.

Once hardened with epoxy to resist concrete pressure during casting, many undercuts in the geometry prevented proper formwork removal. A rubber casting technique was introduced as an intermediary step for easy demoulding. This extra step made the process more cumbersome and less conducive to being scaled up. Column _4 eliminated that hurdle by inventing a flexible device in the formwork itself that could circumvent undercut issues in formwork removal and streamline the formwork making process into fewer steps: negative to positive only, as opposed to positive with fabric, to negative with rubber, to positive again with concrete.

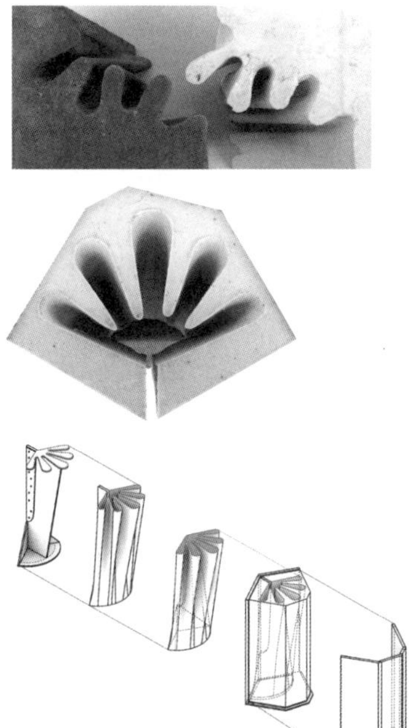

Fig. 36-38: Positive rubber formwork of second iteration to bypass undercut created by the geometry.

Material Accentuations

Concrete is often considered a homogeneous material, a general unifier of one scale. In contrast, New Orders investigates gradual nuances across three main operative scales and their mutual integration, from the overall mass of a column (object) to intermediary concrete pronunciations (tectonic) to local accentuations (detail). Concrete is also known to be a strongly performing compressive material, while weak in tension, which is the reason to compensate with steel reinforcement. Compression as an accumulative force is more passive, giving little possibility for material amplification, but tension does more, in the way it can emit forces, i.e., projecting something onto a space. The prototyping work in formwork searches for these types of material pronunciations in order to make a space more active, without falling for heroic gestures such as an exaggerated cantilever, with everything such an isolated act of bravura might do to a project. Instead, it begins with the treatment of material surfaces beyond mere texturing, questioning how far it can challenge the articulation of its massing through deep voids and changes in thicknesses. By capturing tension in the concrete columns, time appears petrified, as if arrested.

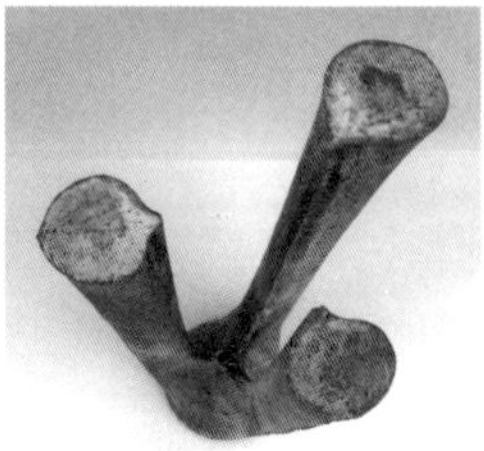

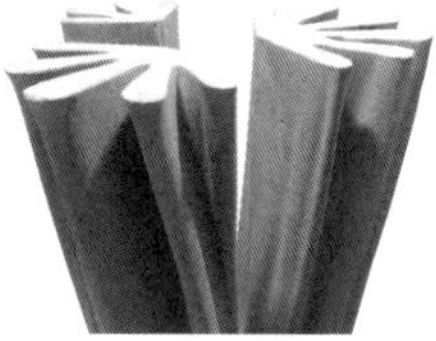

Fig. 39-41: Column_2 overall branching column idea, to corrugation detail study.

Formwork Effects

Some of the spatial qualities and formal language sought after with concrete are revealed precociously within the space of intermediary formworks. They disclose an inner spatiality rendered zonal, evanescent and uninterrupted by edges, appropriate to material fluidity in providing continuity, such as smooth transition between tectonic elements: column to beam. Our other projects are currently pursuing this kind of characteristic. Liquid concrete flows, regardless of types of formwork, whether poured in a rigid box or inside a loose bag, it acts the same; it simply follows its course until it is contained. As long as weight, pressure and leakages are resisted, concrete does not care about formwork. Once solid, it can become everything, anything and nothing. New orders within its scope of enterprise, acknowledge the material's distinct properties. In doing so, they attempt to elevate what the material can really do against more mundane construction practices that have, broadly speaking, normalised concrete and dissociated its full potential from formwork applications, in service of ease of use and low technology required for greater economic returns. By experimenting with a range of formwork procedures, the columns put forward a repertoire of

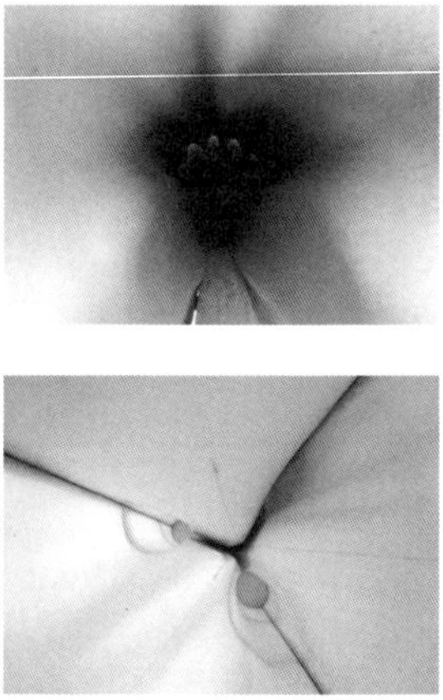

Fig. 42: Looking inside two formwork iterations of column_2 prototyping.

revived techniques, specific to the material behavior. The formworks developed in column_2 try to almost render the concrete amorphous; a frozen fluid shaped only by flow and forces.

Column Inhabitation

The column's spatial and living occupation is investigated on three fronts. First, at the scale of the column, its overall mass is dissected in chunks of sub-massing to identify and reveal key zones of typological differences. These then begin to suggest various types of living arrangements and programmatic distributions, e.g., from semi-public to semi-private to private. Based on this study, a typical or ideal plan diagram is scrutinised and worked out in more detail, its scale reworked to incorporate a range of well distributed living types. Some of the key living units are then extracted and further developed as unit type propositions. Although the living propositions for the columns are relatively speculative, they allow testing of the robustness of their massing and structural principles to internally shape the kinds of living spaces emerging, as well as their agility to create various types and sizes of units. In the case of column_2, its main spatial and structural device is a ribbon wall diverging outwards, vis-à-vis the column's bulk. By undulating in and out of the mass, it delimits an alternation of formally internalised and informally externalised spaces of varying depths, of which each unit makes use. They differ in types and sizes based on the numbers of lobes they are made of, e.g., from studio to three-bedroom unit.

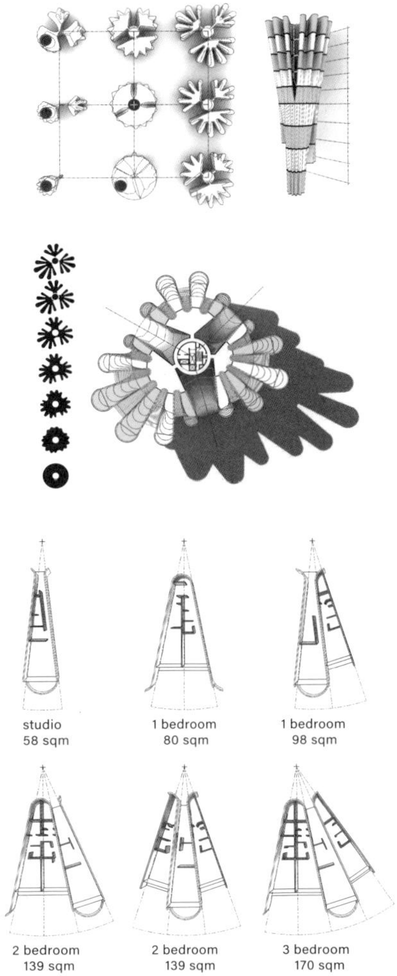

Fig. 43-45: Diagrams of differentiated mass for living, typical plan layout and units' size studies.

Ground Control

The different feet at the bottom of the splitting column are agile in their potential to receive an irregular and sloping ground at various heights, which in turn activates a public space at grade. Each column sits on a wooden base, demarcating specific abstractions of the ground. A dialogue is created between the massing of each column above and the proposition of its conceptual

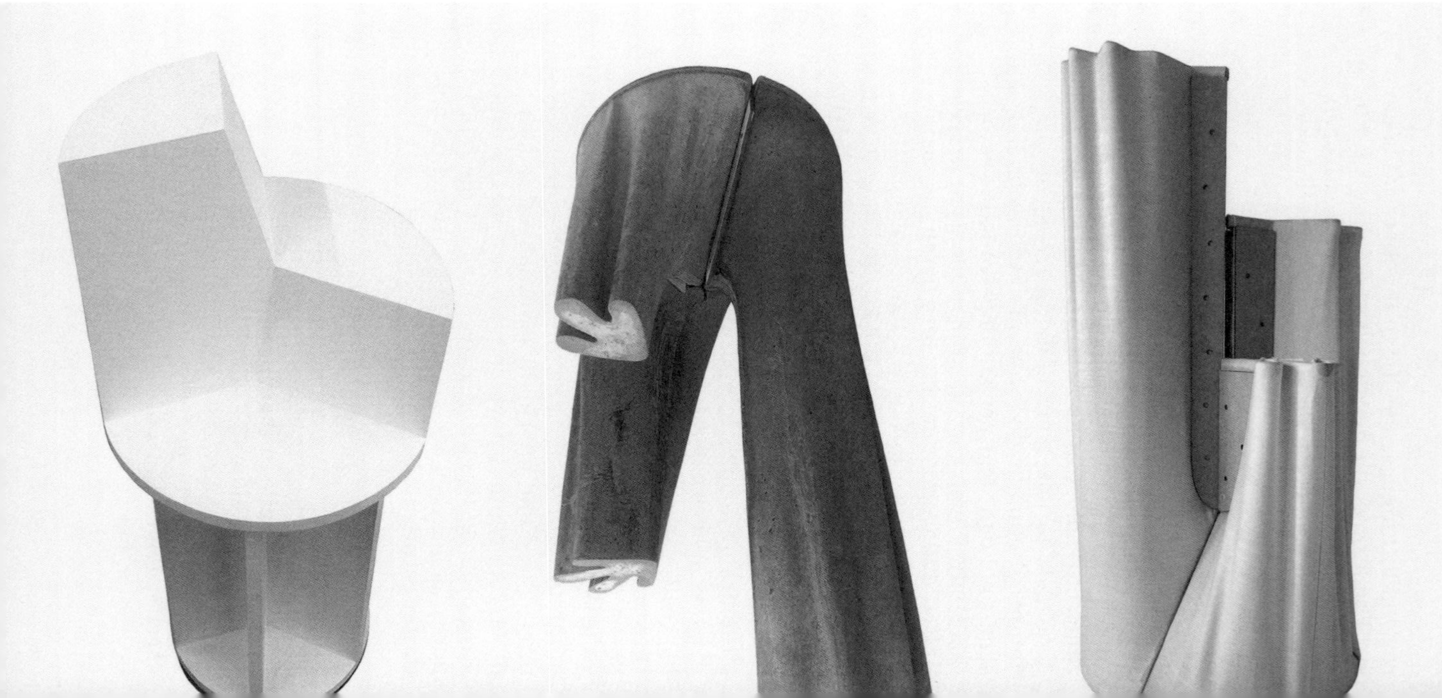

Fig. 46: Ground strategy, concrete cast and formwork.

ground below. Incidentally, the supporting bases become an essential feature of the design of the columns, where the guiding geometry of each column transfers and reacts to the base and vice versa. Being small objects, by default they have ground extensions as bases, helping make the columns less self-referential and therefore less freestanding objects, as is often the case with fabricated artifacts.

The issue of grounding is an important consideration in the work; more so with the way in which larger architecture projects are able to construct a three-dimensional and physical concept of ground for themselves that goes beyond accommodating the literal ground of a site, but instead interacts with the following projects' spatial strategy. The concept of ground plays out more consciously in triggering a spatial displacement, animating the interior of the house Casa Trevo.

Methodology

The benefit of mixing methods in the prototypical ways of making the columns firstly allows us to interrogate early hypotheses from multiple vantage points and through different media simultaneously, and then identify which ones are most significant in driving the process of each column. It was found in fact that the design trajectories varied considerably from column to column, and that if the process was made more linear and top down, unforeseen opportunities would simply not have come to light during the development of the project. Each method presented above provides a specific lens, clarifying their order of importance; for each column, what to concentrate on, and where to let go. The various tropes presented for column_2 are not inclusive; other columns have other fields of investigation, such as, for example, structural analyses in column_1, or environmental analyses through solar radiation studies in column_4. In general, they all operate on different fronts and at different stages in the process, which in turn expands the discovery space for design and the range of techniques for the toolbox.

The more methods at one's disposal, the more agile the process and the more protracted the outcomes.

Ways of Making

Formwork prototyping is the core driver of the project. Concrete casting only gives feedback on the formwork's ultimate performance. Thus, most of the investment is placed into the creation of these temporary constructs to challenge and try to anticipate what liquid concrete can ultimately become. To this effect, it is important that the making process is non-direct, that it involves a few steps for the different formwork materials to be able to interact with one another. It is also essential that the process remains incomplete and not prescribed in terms of the information being transferred from digital models to physical prototypes. The aim is to allow materials to have a final say on the concrete outcomes in less predicted ways: a mediation between an affirmed top-down design and a responsive bottom-up process.

A few contrasting formwork techniques demonstrate how different guiding geometries, such as developable and minimal surfaces, are translated to physical formworks and how some are utilised as form finding devices, attained through computing with a range of materials and their respective properties. Each formwork invented is reusable to facilitate multiple casts. They are conceived in parts, not just for easier formwork removal, but also in search of more volumetrically pronounced effects of cast pieces. Two contrasting formwork techniques are further explained below via selected formworks.

Analogue Computation

The method rationalises three-dimensional curvilinear geometries into frameworks of simple two-dimensional profiles from which sheets of textile optimally interpolate the overall three-dimensional negative space for volume casting. The formwork technique employs a simple means

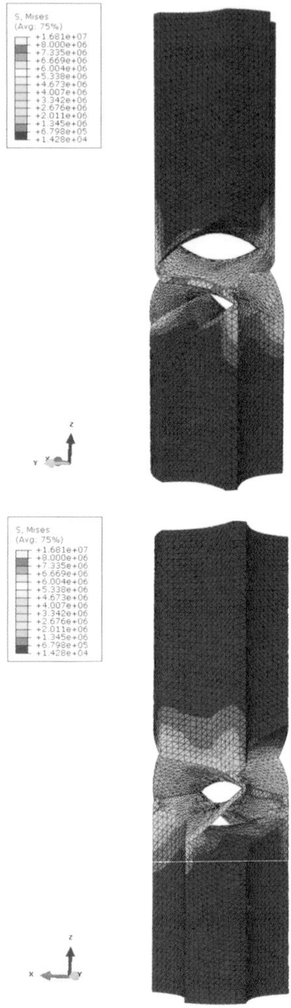

Fig. 47: Structural analysis for column_1's central void.

. 48: Examples of formwork techniques being explored for the ting of the columns.

to fabricate complex geometries. We found to be more effective in deriving an optimised form description than existing cumbersome processes concerned with the copy of digital form into rigid and lost formwork, i.e., plaster copy or CNC (computerized numerical control) milled parts. Once properly secured onto the timber framework, the fabric is then hardened with epoxy coating, ready to be cast. We incrementally experimented with improved versions of this technique in the making of subsequent column prototypes.

In general, the fabric technique, developed incrementally throughout some of this prototyping exercise, is not dissimilar to an effective method invented in the sixteenth century by Philibert de l'Orme, called stereotomy. This art of stone carving made efficient use of projective geometry, by translating spatially complex solids into two-dimensional templates to guide the stone cutter in the carving of a block[10]. Likewise, in the project, the invented formwork method does not require pre-defining the three-dimensional form of an object. It is robust and relatively unlimited in its capacity to describe a large spectrum of volumetric forms, sometimes difficult to model digitally. Eventually, the tensile forces captured by the stretched fabric on the timber frame are extended and rendered active in the concrete outcomes of the columns. They transmit a character of augmented materiality through emissive forces; an active property equally difficult to emulate from digital and/or computed models.

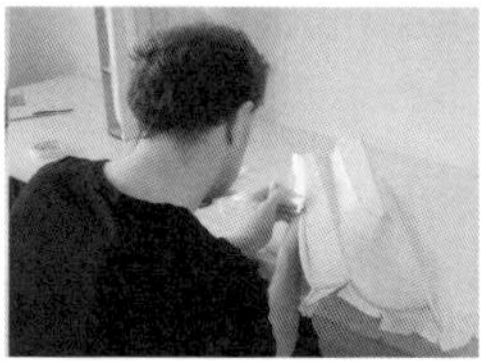

Fig. 49-51: Hands-on approach to an initial formwork made of fabric stretched on wooden frame; a prototype testing column_2's global geometry.

10 Evans, R. 1995. Drawn Stone. *The Projective Cast, Architecture and its Three Geometries*: pp. 179-92. The MIT Press, Cambridge.

Digital Stereotomy

Another form of stereotomy was developed for the making of column_ 8 and column_9. Based on digital protocols of motions of a line describing developable surfaces and volumes of revolution, the technique makes use of a homemade five-axis automated hot wire cutter to section blocks of EPS foam into part-moulds for concrete casting. Forms in the two columns were never literally designed or modelled. Instead, they emerged through the making of the formwork itself, directed by two

Fig. 52-54: Formwork prototype for the testing of a form finding technique: wooden armature, with stretched fabric and three-part mould assembly.

Fig. 55-57: Examples of cut foam pieces from homemade five-axis automated hot wire (developed with Victor Leung), used for mould making and as a design tool.

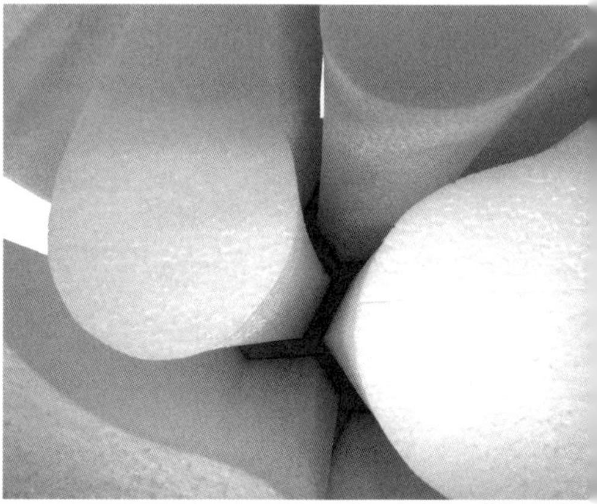

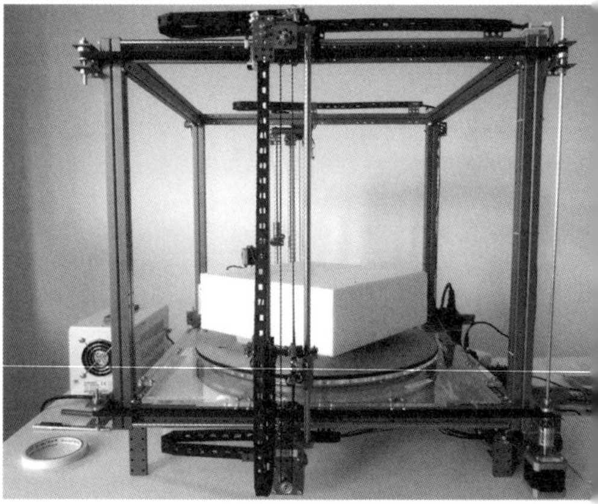

variables: the time and movement of a straight line in space.

The path of the hot wire in space and time dissects a block demarcated by ruled surfaces, e.g., curved surfaces made from a series of straight lines and developable in such a way that they can be unfolded and projected flat. The wire cutting is constant, which brings an aspect of continuity to the description of the foam pieces, corresponding with some of the original intent in working with the concrete material. This prototyping technique is perceived as geometry in its purest physical act. In some ways, it is the most direct formwork procedure invented in the project, and the most open-ended in terms of concrete outcomes. In fact, it became a streamlined design tool for the last two columns of the series and beyond.

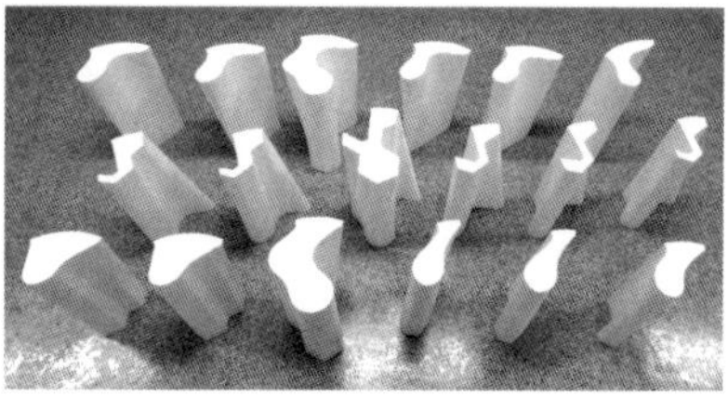

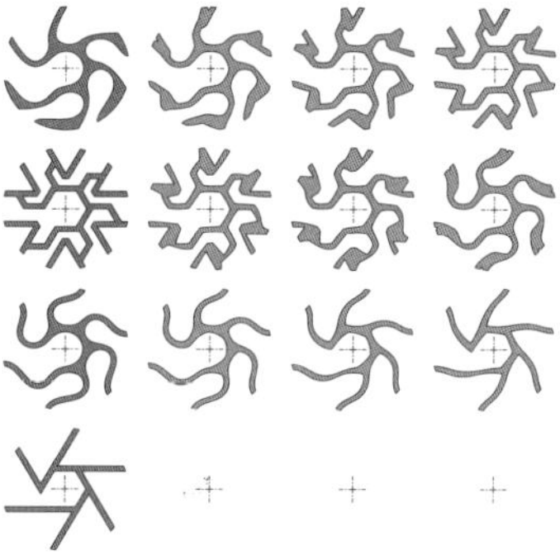

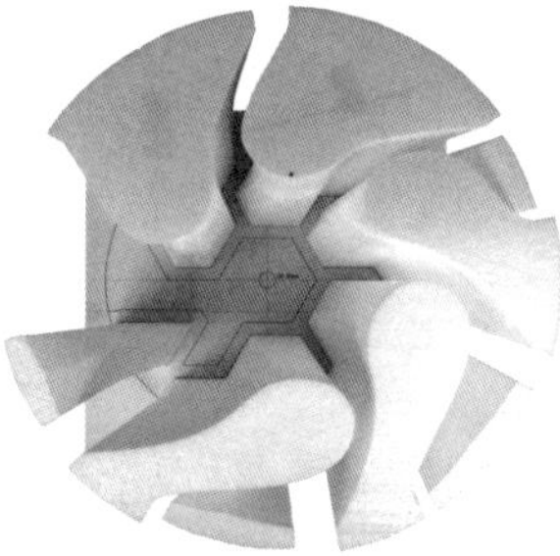

Fig. 58-60: The moulds for column_8, series of horizontal sections of changing profiles and mould prototype assembly for one section.

In column_8, the hot wire cutter takes care of deriving the resulting ruled geometry, linking different horizontal sections identified within the shaft of the column. Taxonomies of EPS-plugs subsequently make up for the negative volumes, in between which the concrete is then poured. In this iteration, time is constant and movement is linear. The technique provides vertical continuity between differentiated profiles in plan. It is fabricated and stacked up in three matching sections. Each section is made of six foam plugs to describe the column's voids.

In column_9, the procedure is extended horizontally. In addition to movement, we introduced a changing time factor. New slab topologies arise from incremental protocols on a moving line in space. Early findings present unique slab topologies, whose forms would have been difficult to preconceive through other means of digital fabrication. Being described by successions of straight lines, these intricate slabs retain an efficient and a direct link to timber formwork and full-scale construction. The mould-making method also resonates with the parallel made above with stereotomy, although this time by operating internally in the carving or slicing of a block. In this instance, time is made irregular and movement non-linear, clockwise and anticlockwise.

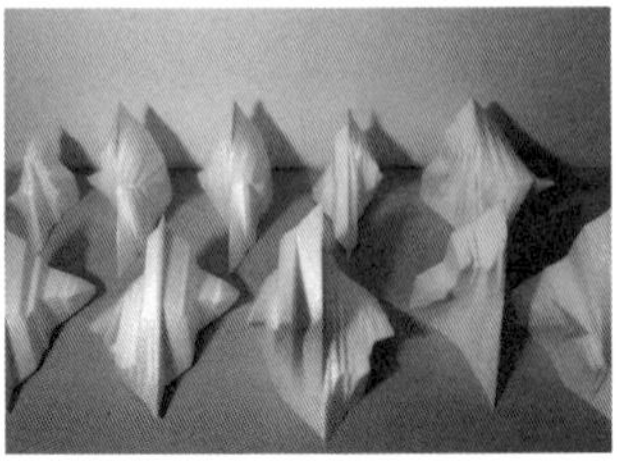

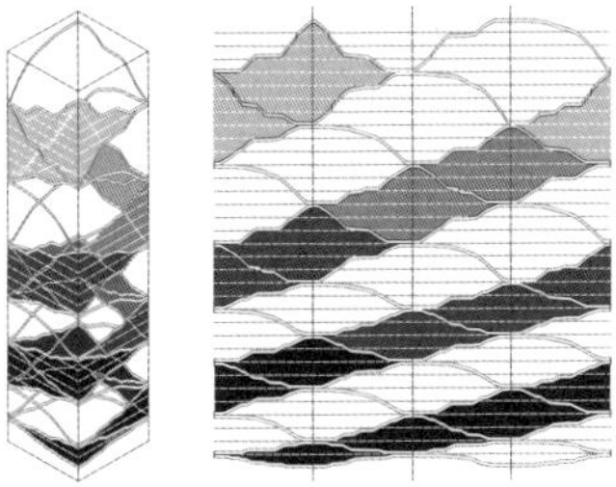

Fig. 61-63: The moulds for column_9, volumetric diagram and map of parts, assembly of mould prototype for one section of the column.

Line on Fire

Early experiments in new slab typologies revealed that more potential existed from this mould-making technique than in the territory covered by the prototyping of the two columns. Hence, the testing continued past the columns themselves as an integral part of the toolbox. There is both a purity and resistance to form-making inherent in the procedure, which is bound to this idea of uncertainty and iteration associated with the work in general.

We used the automated hot wire as the tool to give instructions that were only time and motion based. This increased the sense of the unknown and discovery from an exploratory process, which in turn allowed for some unexpected outcomes to be further directed from iterative feedbacks. Once a foam block was sectioned internally into various pieces, slight displacements were created between them, to allow just enough space for the liquid material to dictate its course. From these displacements, the various cast pieces embodied changes in thicknesses that were a direct registration of the irregular line paths incising the different volumetric pieces. These resulting effects transferred another form of material amplification in their own right, which a slab or shell with even material thickness would not be able to emulate.

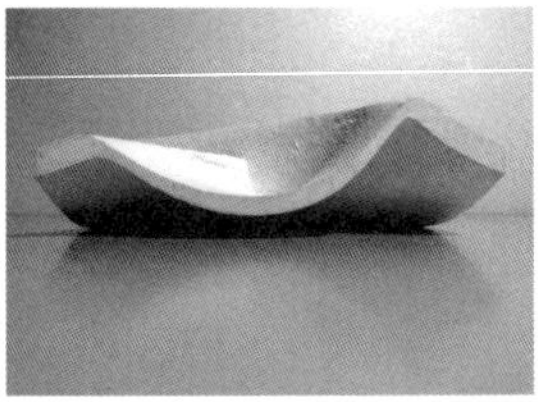

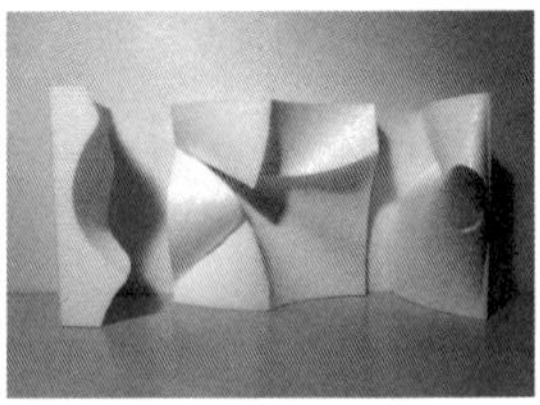

Fig. 64-65: Slab emerging from moulds described by a moving straight line.

Iterative Process

New Orders comprises nine successive iterations of concrete columns. The columns can be mixed in different orders based on diverse research aspects and priorities: these comprise the toolbox. They interchange ideas and concepts and crossbreed prototyping techniques, remaining open to further developments in seeding new work. In fact, the collection of concrete tests produced during the making of each column remains the most productive aspect of the iterative procedure adopted for the project. Each test is a focused yet open experiment, incrementally addressing more variables in order to hierarchically direct its prototyping process. The value of working at 1:1 scale lies in computing with materials proactively and in the empirical feedback given from active forces of materials to direct a process of design opportunity to new research findings as they occur. The iterative process is a necessity for the idea of prototyping and it is something that runs across all the work.

Serial Outcome

In the column series, common themes run through several columns, explored through different massing strategies and formwork techniques. For example, column_3, column_4 and column_5 are concerned with the articulation of a central void or courtyard space, introducing interiority to the shaft. In column_4, the void is delineated by a thick and monolithic wall, semi-open on its periphery. In column_3, the inner voided space is demarcated by four slender elements connected in a ring mid-height while forking at the base to create a lighter footprint. In column_5, the voided shaft is bounded by an aggregation of modular elements whose corners' connections are left open to produce a family of sub-voids, perforating the thickened circular envelope.

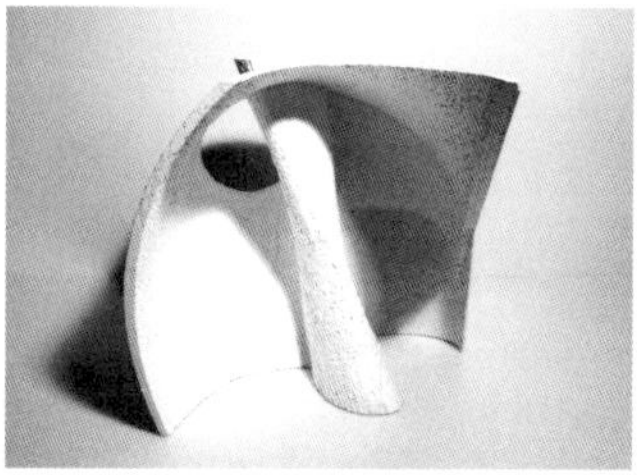

Fig. 66-68: Cast volume made from mould pieces described from a moving straight line.

Other themes specific to columns are: the perforating of the shaft of column_1 through shelling to open a semi-public space mid-air; the cracking of the mass of column_9 to create terraced spaces ascending around its perimeter; the splitting of column_ 8 through profiling to generate internal shaded spaces of different depths; the sieving of the mass of column_7 through fluting to disclose an ambiguity between indoor and outdoor spaces, and so on. Each column concept is defined by a sequence of actions that hold architectural consequences in organising space through massing methods and material processes.

The general intention of the series is to define grades of operative scales within each column, i.e., large voids dissolving into smaller voids, capable of differentiating their overall massing while maintaining a sense of continuity and monolithic reading intrinsic to the concrete material. In general, each column explores different sizes of mass and void as place holders, further guiding their spatial organisation and programmatic distribution at a scale of 1:100. The dialogue in the design process between scales of 1:1 and 1:100, shaping each column's final built proposition, does not occur in a linear manner, e.g., 1:1 dictating 1:100. Rather, various forms of feedback between the two scales occur back and forth during the making of each. In that regard, the columns are both materially and spatially driven.

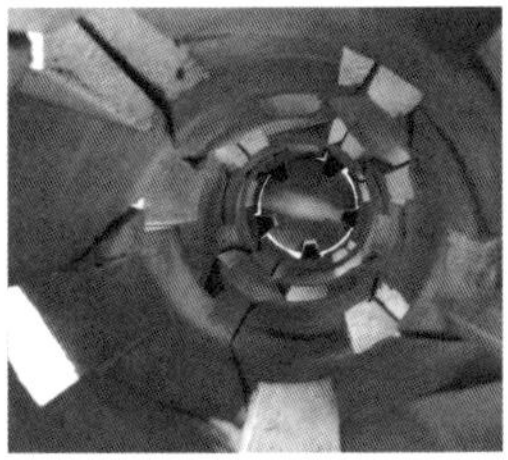

Fig. 69-71: Three iterations on a central void from column_3, column_4 and column_5.

The advantage of working in series exists in its comparative reading. None of the columns stands alone or operates in isolation from the others. They are evolutionary in the manner that sets of ideas are being tested differently in several columns, with their premises also transforming and evolving from column to column. Although distinctive in appearance, they form a family of concepts and techniques which remains open-ended and still capable of further offspring. In essence, they are iterative vis-à-vis one another; they cross-breed each other in a non-chronological order.

Another form of serial reading takes place in the emerging language of some of the columns themselves. For example, the peripheral voids of column_5 are demarcated by various combinations of tiles, ranging from three to eight. Consequently, they offer a lexicon of possibilities to materialise types of voided spaces, rather than relying on a singular and repetitive solution. The voids' index discloses a taxonomy that is relational and not limited.

Iterative Approach

Iterations also played an important role in the prototyping process of each column's formation.

72: Examples of incremental testing of concrete casts.

Many tests were carried out incrementally in the making of the columns. They start small and focus on the main massing idea in working with concrete. A large part of the discovery originates from the formwork itself. Devising formworks with a range of different materials, processes and geometries is the uncertain factor in the work, as far as concrete is concerned. Some tests led nowhere or became too forceful, others failed or were mistargeted, but some results turned out quite unexpected and instrumental in shaping some of the design trajectories. All, nonetheless, remained part of a toolbox that could be used for future applications, transformations or revisions. In this iterative approach, once a trajectory has been defined and an initial technique mastered, the incremental tests become larger in size and more ambitious in nature, until a column has reached its full formation, after which the exploration shifts to another column. Working in this way has several benefits. First, the process is very productive, creating unforeseen and alternative tracks of research for future work. In other words, it is divergent, rather than convergent. It also foregrounds the concrete material and its counterpart, the formwork, as the live catalysts through which new forms of spatial organisations are made possible. Lastly, the most important aspect to emerge from this type of work was the relation of mass to scale; or the way an idea of mass triggers a positive distortion of scale, e.g., how big or small something appears. This nuance is further exploited in the Casa Trevo project and discussed in the next chapter.

Inhabiting Scales

New Orders was inspired in part by the work of some of the 'structural mavericks' mentioned previously. However, it departs from precedents in its direct response to the high-rise urban context of Hong Kong, China. At 1:100 scale, the columns are further tested as speculative towers for vertical living. In contrast to Hong Kong, China's normalised housing tower blocks, in which living has become individualised after the pattern of

Fig. 73-77: Taxonomy of void openings in column_5, defined by different numbers of aggregations of concrete tiles around each sub-opening.

78: The New Orders towers in their intended Hong Kong, ıa context against the city's existing built fabric.

the Dom-Ino prototype, the columns search for new point-block diagrams that are more agile in transiting from one type of program to another. They aim to provide residents with a range of living styles and gradients of communal spaces that reconcile with (semi-) outdoor living qualities desirable in a sub-tropical climate. This is achieved from drawing analyses that cut the columns into sub-categories of differentiated living masses, e.g., scales within scales, whose internal units' organisations are further interrogated in plan and section. Programming the columns into specifically distributed living entities occurs in conjunction and back and forth with the 1:1 scale concrete prototyping for greater design integration. Building structures for residential high-rise tend to be homogenous in scale. In the context of Hong Kong, China where land is scarce and expansive, besides an effort placed on the articulation of (semi-) public podium at ground level, the living complexes above often constitute repetitions of same scale living units, uninterrupted across heights. New orders search for ways to disrupt the homogeneity of scale within tower complexes and further speculates on mixed organisations of living types, catering to a mixture of social classes, as opposed to assigning a building type to its specific class, i.e. high-end vs. low-cost housing.

Each column investigates a different living strategy from an initial massing, varying in height and in plan. This is informed by the unique properties given from prototyping with the concrete material and formworks techniques. Early in the process, the columns are sequentially sectioned horizontally or vertically to reveal their effectiveness or shortcomings in supporting a range of kinds and sizes of living typologies. In most columns, a typical plan chosen from a series of horizontal sections is developed at an early stage and benchmarked against the others to assess the extent of spatial differentiation a column's massing can provide. Based on the results, it is revised, transformed and recalibrated through iterations along with the development of the 1:1 column prototype. Subsequently, volumetric studies are

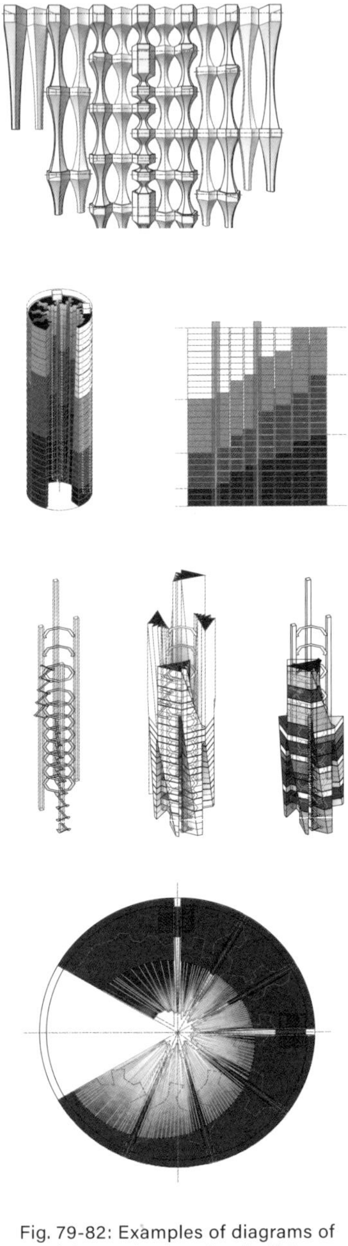

Fig. 79-82: Examples of diagrams of spatial organisations for the living towers.

conducted by diagramming clusters of different types of living units along with their distribution and access within the tower mass. Public to private thresholds are also established. The towers' relationships to ground and sky, e.g., how they begin and finish, are also considered an important conceptual aspect of the project in transiting from material object: column; to contextualised spatial entity: tower.

Scale-wise, the towers divulge a sense of monumentality at times, exaggerated by their response to gravity. Their representational thicknesses, at 1:100 scale, are off when seen against more conventional types of structures for high-rise. They are not scaled models, but prototypes performing at their intended size. The misfit is somewhat embraced, considering their degree of abstraction coming from the column scale at 1:1. A critical distance is maintained about the represented reality the towers should convey, even though some of the gaps in scale translation are addressed by diagrammatic and analytical drawings. A key discovery in working at two scales simultaneously was in the ambiguity or close proximity massing concepts had on structure and spatiality. Merging the three suddenly became a possibility; one where mass turns void to become habitable structure. This aspect was further put to test in the design of the Casa Trevo house.

Conclusion

The work presented in this chapter is still very much alive and continues to inform new work. In this regard, it is not conclusive, but rather conducive to further explorations. The ambition with New Orders was to create a toolbox of formwork techniques and concrete languages informed by the material's fluidity that could impact new projects. New Orders made an effort in reviving and (re-) elevating the virtue of working actively with the liquid material. It also investigates the relationship between material experimentations and projections of space, to discover their interdependencies and degrees of influences over one another. The columns, we found, are in the end as much spatial as they are material.

The columns series is experimental in its aspiration to search for alternative ways of thinking about larger construction methods with the material rather than conforming to more generic and monotonous building applications, such as those found in the construction industry today, i.e., the ubiquitous concrete frame dictating many building scales. The invention lies in how something is made, e.g., construction procedures, rather than in the preoccupation with the final object as a formal product. The project also resists situating any design decisions in the digital realm only. The columns are relatively small-scale and much of the prototyping preoccupation was placed on form-finding strategies with formwork design and their materiality. The project exploits the gap between digital processes and physical constructs as a productive space for discoveries, where geometry is an important link between the two. A very productive finding in the New Orders project was its misalignment in scale; that is in the columns' relationship of mass to scale. They are material and spatial, yet the gap between the two is pertinent to scale. To cast something in concrete requires a minimum mass, volume and thickness, otherwise it breaks into bits upon demoulding. Because the columns are only of a certain size, their overall massing is out of proportion vis-a-vis their intended reading at the scale of inhabitation. This, in effect, boosted their volumetric and mass perception, making them not quite fit the observer's potential reference with reality. Little of this characteristic was exploited until the design of the house project Casa Trevo, which plays much more with collisions of scales and mass and their subsequent perception. In terms of design methods for prospective work, New Orders was instrumental in conditioning the architectural intentions of the house Casa Trevo presented in the next section. It demonstrates how a process geared towards prototyping can nourish the design process of larger architecture projects, even though their constructions are

Fig. 83-86: Spectrum of architectural language and synopsis of massing concepts framed for each column as architecture grammar feeding new projects.

somewhat dissociated from the encompassing process of the project by being delegated to independent contractors.

Fig.1: Bird's-eye view of house in its natural context.

TREFOIL HOUSE / CASA TREVO – THREE PATIOS FOR THE SUN: PRELUDE

Casa Trevo or Trefoil House is a two-storey residence located south of Lisbon, Portugal. The site's close proximity to the Atlantic Ocean provides pleasant breezes and plenty of sunshine across all seasons. The project sits in a forest of pine trees, rising tall above a sandy terrain.

Inside, the rooms are organized around three outdoor patios, circular in shape. They function as extensions of the interior spaces, as well as being light wells and large openings for the living quarters below and sleeping rooms above.

The 9m-high patios also perform as main structural voids in the form of three hollowed and semi-open columns. Together, they support a series of floor slabs ascending at different increments. They also hold a beam of water, serving as a lap pool on the rooftop and whose underbelly presses down on the spaces below.

The structure is made of cast-in-place concrete and plays off the ambiguity of mass and void, and of inside and outside. It addresses the site by stepping the ground plane along its natural slope and by bringing that level difference inside. It is anchored into the ground firmly but irregularly around its perimeter vis-à-vis the terrain.

Casa Trevo exerts a peculiar sense of autonomy and monumentality, despite its small size. It is unified by concrete on the outside, subverting the perception of its scale, while serving as canvas on which a dialogue between nature and architecture can be projected. It further exudes a solid impression of mass, at the same time revealing little of its inside. The house produces its own introverted world facing the sun, with private yet mutable spaces rendered intermittently by Lisbon's brash sunlight.

Design Summary

The house is organised in a trefoil arrangement, sitting on three columns, hence its name Casa Trevo or Trefoil House. The outdoor patios are the trefoil elements, supporting the bulk of the rounded house above ground. The patios are structural voids, subtracted from the overall mass. The position towards the site was to visually negate it, while physically impacting it. The house does so visually by blocking most horizontal views outwards and by opening up vertically to allow the sky in with much natural sunlight.

Some of the key moves which will be further explained in the various sections below are: to lift the mass off the ground; to insert the program below; to introduce a new ground as roof-scape; to introduce three hollow columns as both structure and space; to suspend a beam of water mid-air; to break and redistribute the horizontal slab; to keep the area of all rooms the same; to differentiate volumes for living; to implement an open and dynamic circulation; to erase all façades; and to integrate essential concrete details.

Concrete is almost the only material in the project, and the reason for using and testing this material is to have material, structure and space become one, performing architecturally as a coherent whole. Internally, space is read as pure subtraction or voided presence. It is also the way the geometry is set in plan, by having overlapping and incomplete figures, between circles and polygons, to accentuate a relative degree of porosity and impermeability of space. We sought a spectrum of physical dualities and temporal ambiguities that could generate multiple types of varied spatial experiences; a test for the house's conceptual longevity. Through its ultimate spatial proposition, the project aims to extend one's preconception of what a house is, towards that which its spatial responsiveness could engender.

Another ambition is a return to what the Dom-ino diagram had previously erased; the dissociation of architecture from structure. Instead, more than just freeing up the plan, the house reclaims the potential for spatial living: an Albert Loos 'Raumplan' of interconnected continual spaces versus a Le Corbusier 'Free Plan'. The incentive in Casa Trevo is to restore and experiment with both concepts at once, assessing what the outcomes might entail, as a case study in synthesising previous research findings (New Orders) and in projecting new ones.

The structural diagram supporting the idea of 'free-plan' or individualisation of space in Le Corbusier's 'Maison Dom-ino' was put to the test in most of his houses. It did so by liberating the architecture, freeing up the horizontal slab datum from its structural imperatives. In the end, the prototype turned out to be so flexible and generic that instead it was universally taken for granted in widely promoting repetition and homogenisation of space. In contrast to the ubiquitous Domino protocol, the concrete columns of New Orders began testing concepts of breaking the horizontal datum of the prototype, as devices to re-animate spatial living. The intention was to reassert individualised and heterogeneous types of volumetric spaces within a structural framework. Early findings were then transferred and put to full effect in the slab dispositions and spatial organisation of the house Casa Trevo.

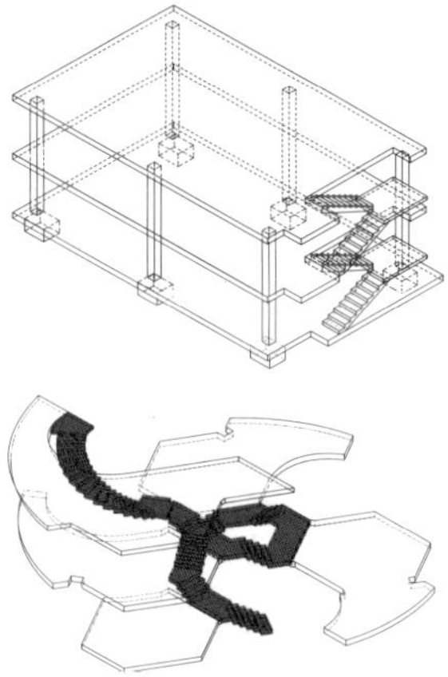

Fig. 2-3: Column-slab stacking system with adjacent circulation of 'Maison Dom-ino' versus the central distribution of the breaking up of the slabs of Casa Trevo.

The project offered the sudden opportunity to test many architectural ideas all at once, the idea being that too many was better than too few. A main design concern was to ensure these ideas and concepts had a properly defined hierarchy or established degree of importance, so that concepts were well-integrated and well-weighted vis-à-vis one another. If not, it would run the risk of creating constant 'white noise'.

Construction Approach

From a constructional standpoint, Casa Trevo is a thorough exploration of cast-in-situ concrete. Therefore, a close scrutiny of formwork design was essential from the onset of the project. It is a relatively unconventional house built in a rather conventional and professionally established building context; one where architecture is culturally valued and broadly discussed. It was clear from the beginning that construction had to be contractually and legally conducted by a chosen independent contractor and his designated sub-contractors, and that my direct approach as maker to some of its building process would have been nullified. This meant that the space for physical experimentation was going to be narrow this time, and had to be more foregrounded in the design process.

To address that issue, we had to question the value and reassess the role of prototyping with active materials, as presented in the New Orders project. Fortunately, the design of the house did not start from scratch, but from extractions and transformations of formerly made concrete prototypes with specific formwork techniques, realised at smaller scales. Once a design proposal for the house matured, the issue became one of building translation. By clearly identifying the key concepts, the challenge was to adjust their methods of construction to the material palette of the contractor without losing track of what their original intentions were. For example, in regards to the weighted hierarchy mentioned before, an important factor was to determine where to strategically concentrate the material focus and effort in the concrete part of the house, such as in devising particular types of formworks for more pronounced concrete expressions, e.g., the circular columns, as well as where to let go of them. In letting go, the detailing approach was to erase details as much as possible, as a means to provide a clear continuity in the treatment of surfaces, in order to maintain a cohesive whole and an uninterrupted reading of the mass across the entire project.

In addition to the construction drawing packages submitted, e.g., engineering and architectural, we made incremental physical models before and during construction to best communicate the primary intentions with the various project team members. Construction started in the spring of 2018 and was completed in March 2020.

Fig. 1: Main relational geometry in base plan and site survey plan of construction of foundations.

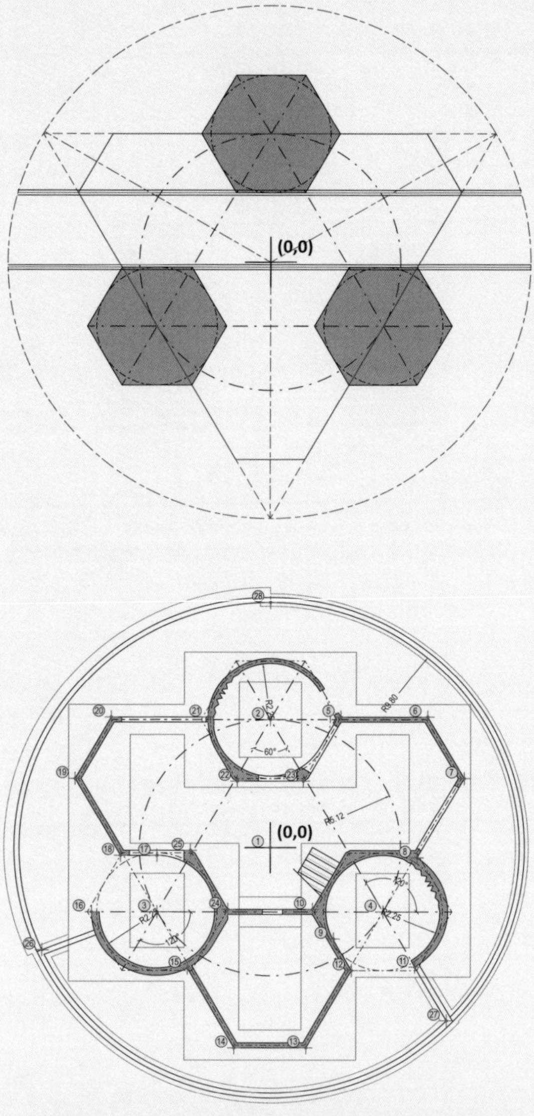

NINE DESIGN PURSUITS

PLAIN GEOMETRY
(on geometry: plan)

The role of geometry in the work is procedural and non-compositional; it is dynamic but not graphic. A relational framework serves as a regulatory plan diagram, a basis from which all parts relate and are integrated into a coherent whole. It is prescribed yet agile in adapting to various design evolutions until a solid formation is reached. The adaptive take on geometry is what facilitates the prototypical aspect of projects, receptive to feedback from engaging with material properties, massing transformations and projecting new building procedures. Having tectonic elements relate to one another allows each design move to have a certain degree of influence on and consequences for the next one. In this respect they are not additive or finite in and of themselves. Instead, the use of geometry becomes associative, allowing changes to occur while continually revising parts-to-whole relationships, in pursuing synthesis.

Three Plan Conditions

The order of the base plan for the house is as follows: the pool (1), the three circular patios tangential to it (2), the four remaining polygonal spaces organised in and around the patios (3). The plan's evenness is deliberate yet flexible to the insertion of a central beam, the pool, of a variable width. A hierarchy is established from outside (1) to outside-inside (2) to inside (3). That is to say, the most formal and functionally defined rooms, e.g., dining, living and kitchen on ground floor, and bedrooms plus bathrooms above, are the residual areas of a pre-established geometrical hierarchy, rendering their clear boundaries indeterminate. The plan diagram is intentionally incomplete, allowing the surrounding nature to filter into the house, and allowing the house's interior to diffuse outwards.

Fig. 2: Excavation, groundwork and retaining wall.

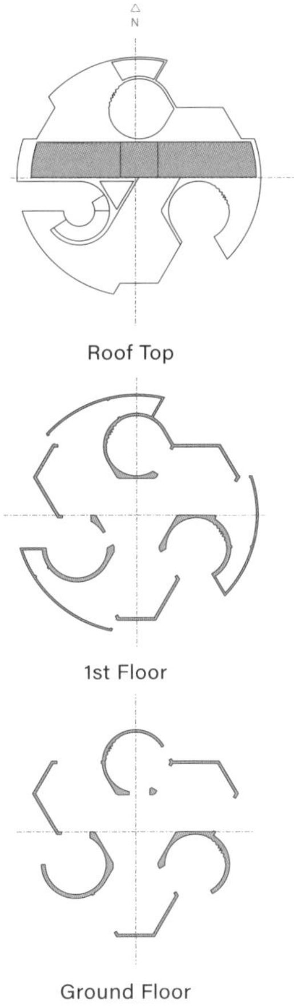

Fig. 3: Plan diagrams.

The aggregation of elements, constituting column_7 of New Orders, was the genesis of the plan for the house. Extractions of inside-outside and mass-void relationships were analysed by a series of sections through the column's concrete massing. Early findings were then examined and further transformed at the scale of the house.

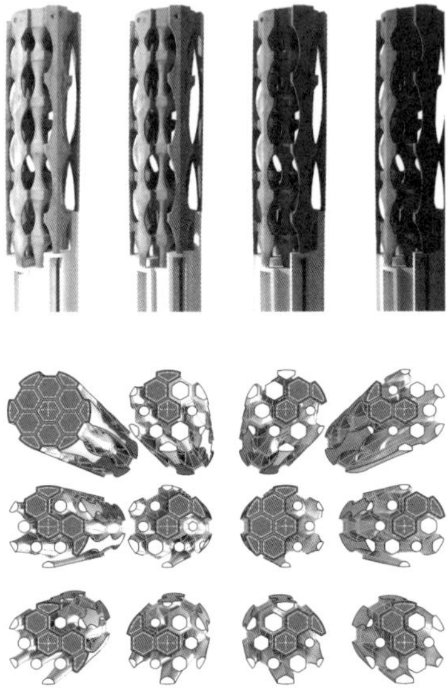

Fig. 4-5: Indoor-outdoor spatial relationships of column_7 and porosity study from horizontal sections through the column shaft.

Ground floor: Outward-looking at ground level, the plan plays with the ambiguity of identical types of spaces in size and shape, leaving the subject wondering about his or her exact position internally. Her or his clear escape is established vertically by height differences. Horizontally, the subject is sandwiched in each room in-between openings to the outside, views across rooms and openings to the semi-enclosed patio spaces. The planning intention for the ground floor is to be evenly distributed while remaining relatively porous; each room visually relates to the others, and opens to outside contexts.

The ground plan comprises seven spaces; three identical outdoor patios, one central hexagonal atrium and three identical indoor hexagonal spaces, e.g., kitchen, dining room and living room. Each one opens on two opposing sides; one full height window facing each patio respectively, the other directed to the open site in different orientations: east, west and south. The ground plan is centrifugal, i.e. extroverted, leaking out, not bounded. It clamps the subject constantly between different readings of space, possibly inciting a sense of 'deja-vu' or recurrence. With a restricted footprint of 160m2 of internal space, the outdoor patios help to spread the footprint wider and make the house seem larger in size. As the proximate site leaks in as much as the house leaks out, it is a numbers game based on the permitted area, tuned to a southern European climate. In summertime, the size of the house expands outwards towards the outdoor spaces, while in the winter it contracts back inwards.

Second floor: In contrast, the second floor is more private and inward-looking. Each of the three bedrooms has access to light, air and views only via their respective patios. These characteristics make these types of spaces more enclosed, introverted and centripetal. The views provided from the bathrooms adjacent to each of the three bedrooms are peripheral, with two openings located at either end of their circular and cantilevering walls; one is a 'meutrière', a narrow and tall window sheared through the house's concrete mass, while the other faces a bottomless lightwell, providing light and privacy for the shower rooms.

Rooftop: The roof terrace has no reference to a single centre. It is somewhat eccentric, or perhaps polycentric, in regards to the three circular and voided spaces that pierce it. It becomes the moment where the structural idea is most legible in plan; a beam of water supported by three voided columns.

In general, the plans appear very composed, but experientially they are absolutely not. One is constantly being circulated around, up and down staircases while facing different views at the same time. It is anything but static. The experiential reading of the resultant space is an interesting contrast and a productive contradiction to the plan itself. The plan diagram of the house only operates as a base, which will never be read in reality. One will just happen to occupy it, consciously or not.

Circled In

The circle is used as a recurring figure throughout the projects. The reason is that it is an easy figure to break away from, while retaining some of its best attributes. Its roundness has continuity and does not privilege any straight sides at the risk of becoming static. It also preconditions several strict properties to be counteracted through design iterations, such as being a complete and hermetic figure, defined by one fixed centre and a constant diameter. When extruded three-dimensionally, e.g., a cylindrical form, it resists any fixed framing by having its surface curvature bending at either end, behind any cones of vision.

Fig. 6: Ground floor plan showing the various living areas.

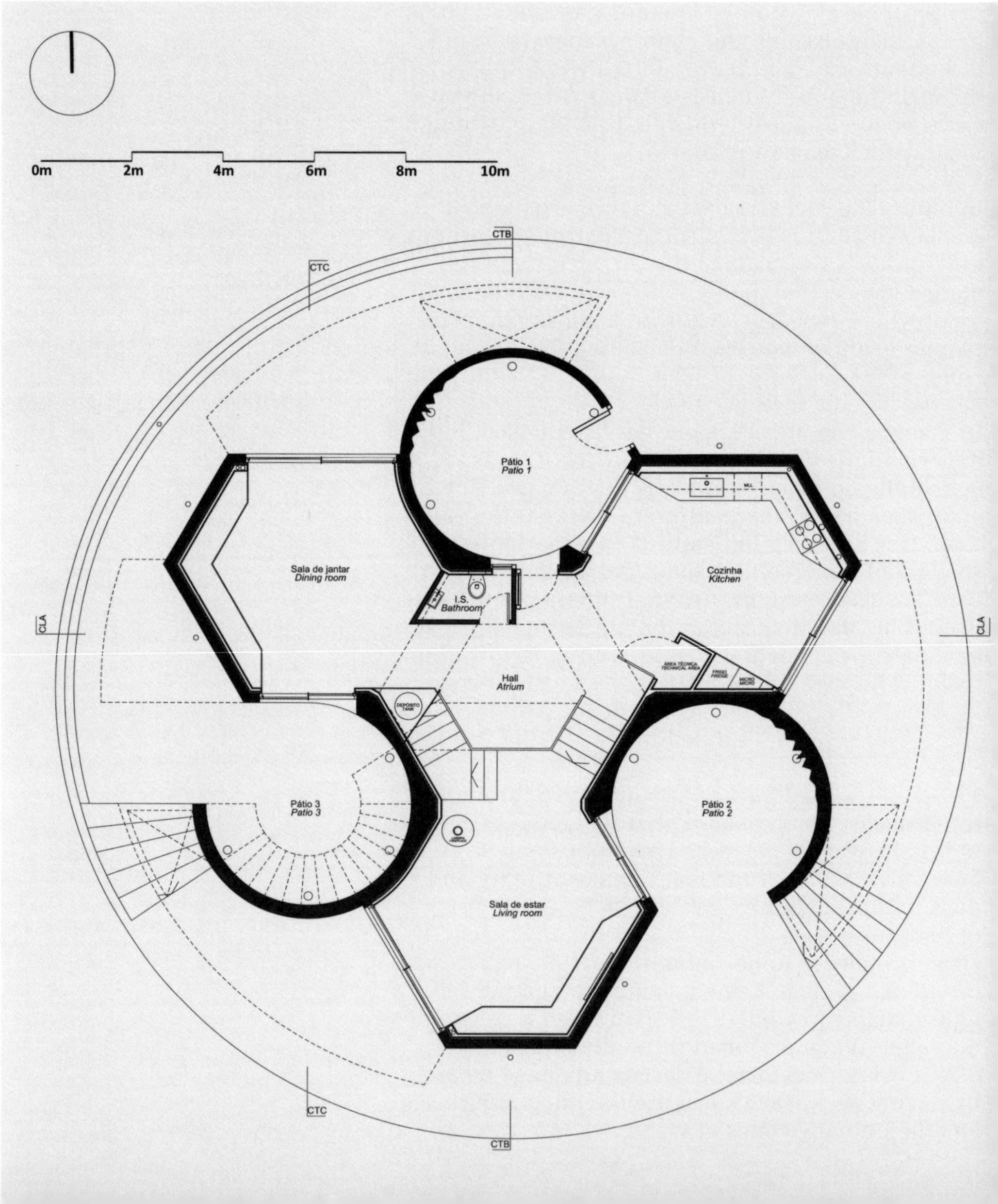

7: First floor showing the sleeping areas.

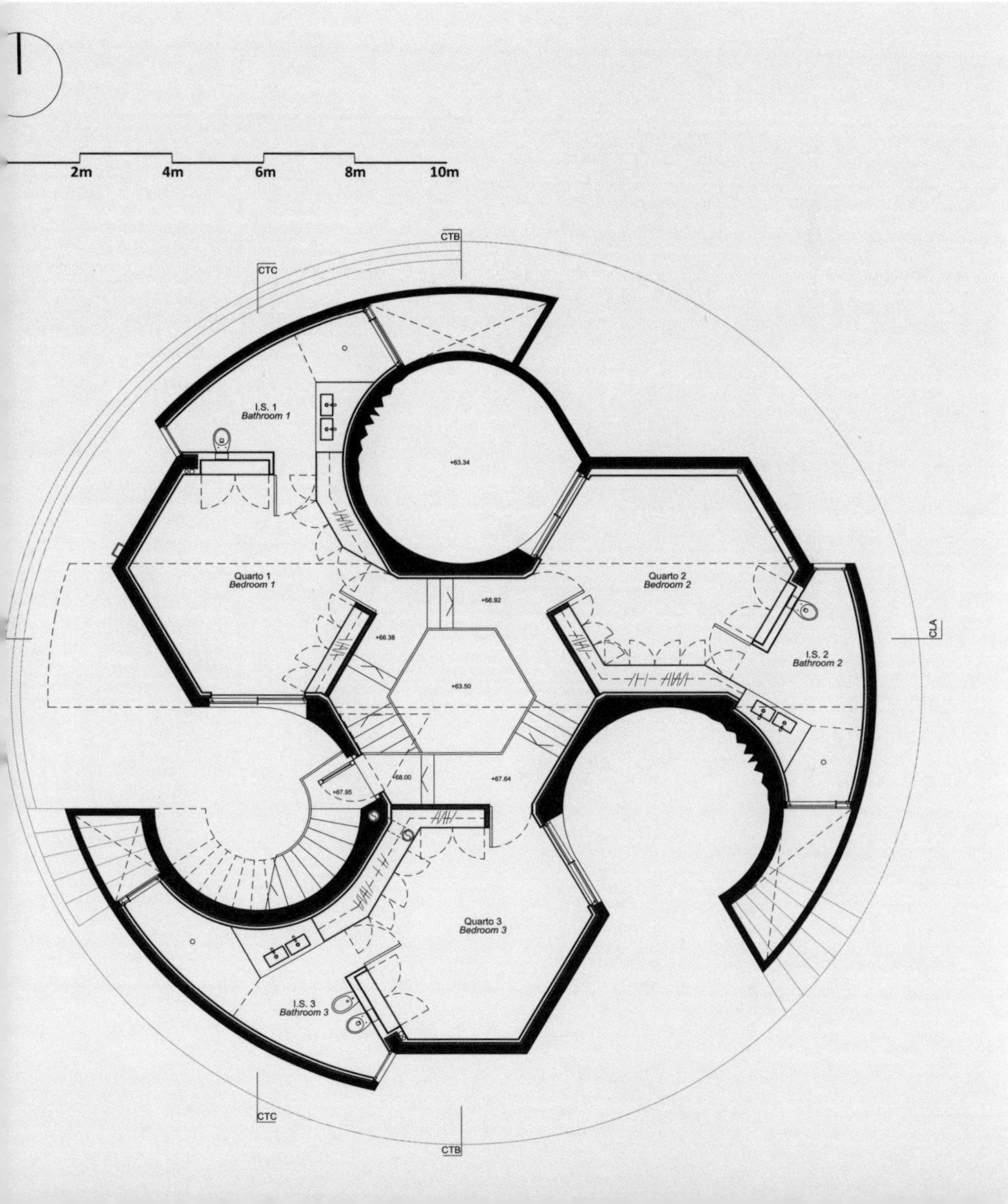

Fig. 8: Roof plan showing the recreational areas.

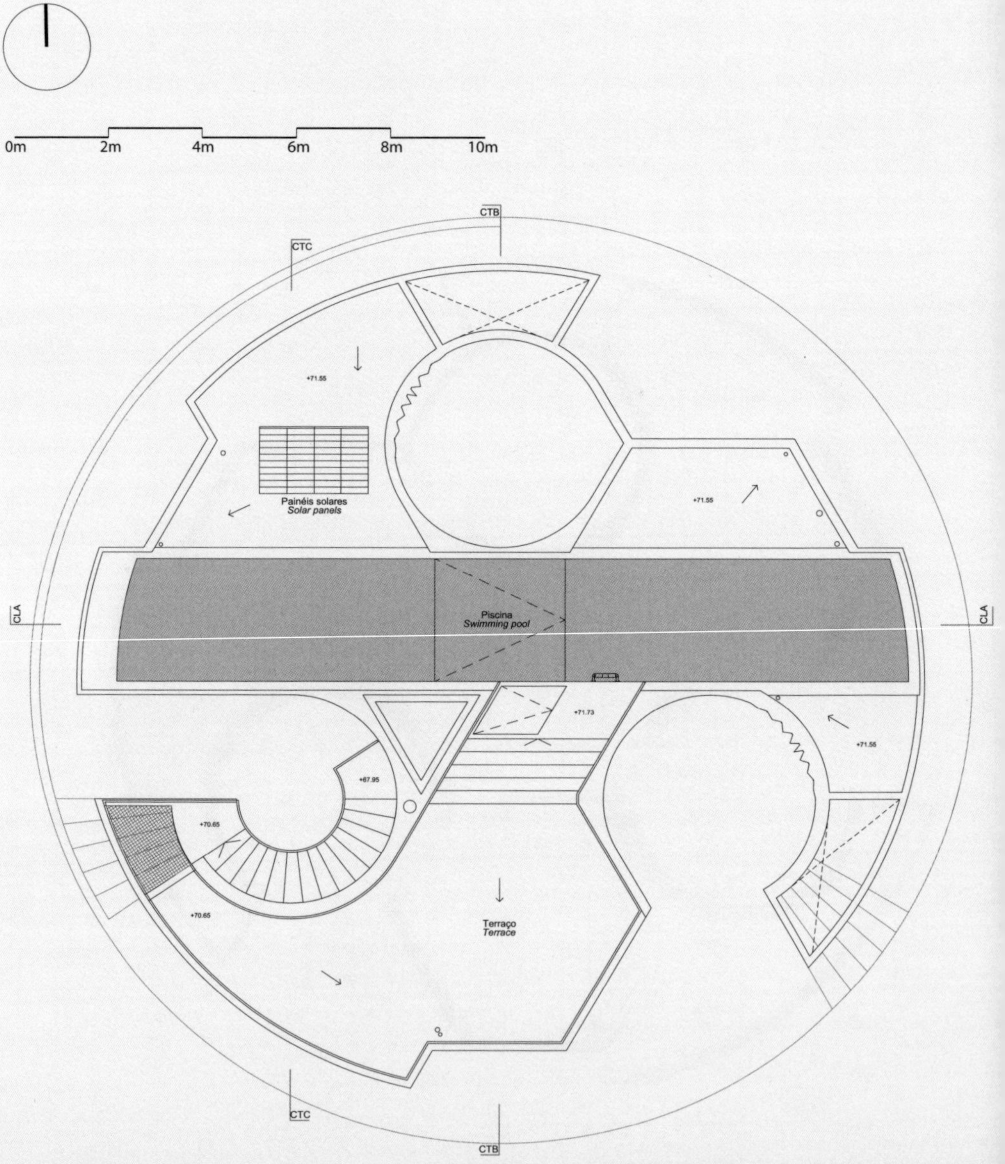

9: Site plan showing a site area of 1,050 square meters inside hexagpnal shape, with a house footprint of around 20 meters meter after required setbacks from site outline.

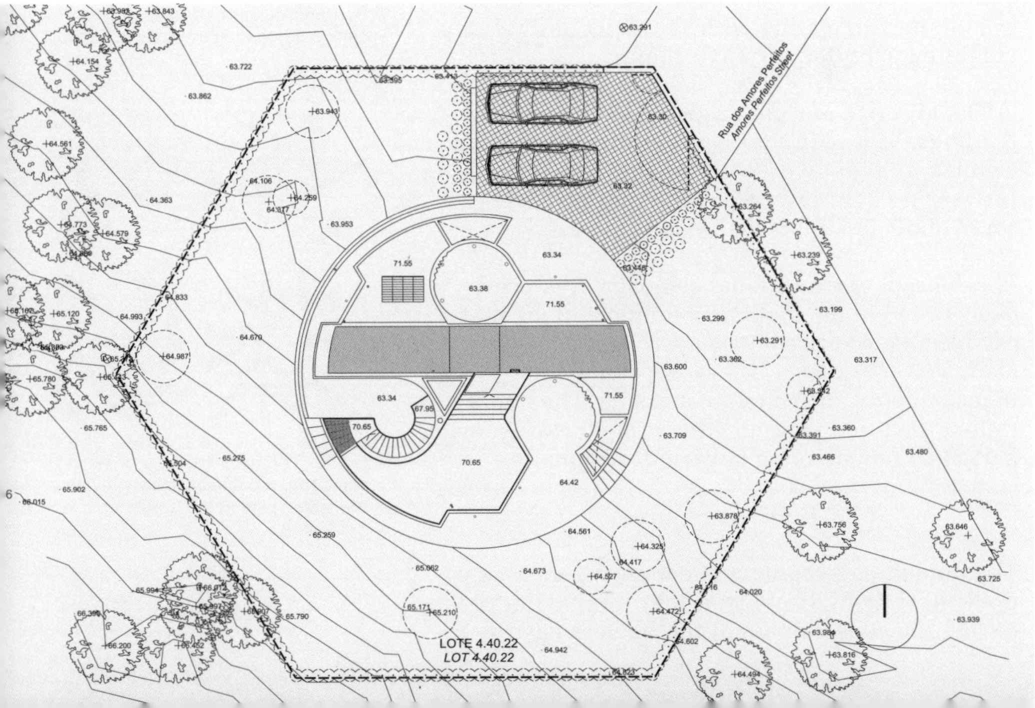

Trefoil Position

To address the issue of the plan of the house being a prescribed composition, a comparative study of Borromini's ceiling outline for the dome of the church of 'Sant'ivo alla Sapienza' in Rome, with the plan diagram of Casa Trevo speaks directly of three common geometrical properties, from which the house's differentiated massing was generated:

a) The dissolution and absorption of key figures between circles and polygons through geometrical operations, such as differences and intersections of shapes of various sizes. The result is the emergence of an incomplete figure, described partially on its periphery and internally to become flexible to different part-to-whole relations, associations and disjunctions in plan.

b) A basic armature from which things can evolve differently above and below: the consequence in the house is a geometrical figure that is transitional in accommodating vertical changes. A series of varied extrusions of elements is then set in motion, correlating with the slabs' different height distribution for each room.

c) The absence of right angles: The outcome in the house is a plan that is multi-directional and cellular, able to diverge out to views as much as converging light inwards, while not privileging a set of static positions vis-à-vis context.

The concept of transitional geometry was previously tested in the making of Column_ 8, by first establishing a series of key open figures in plan along its vertical axis. These were then interpolated to make up for the concrete massing. The house rationalised that concept with straight extrusions of partial figures merging at various heights.

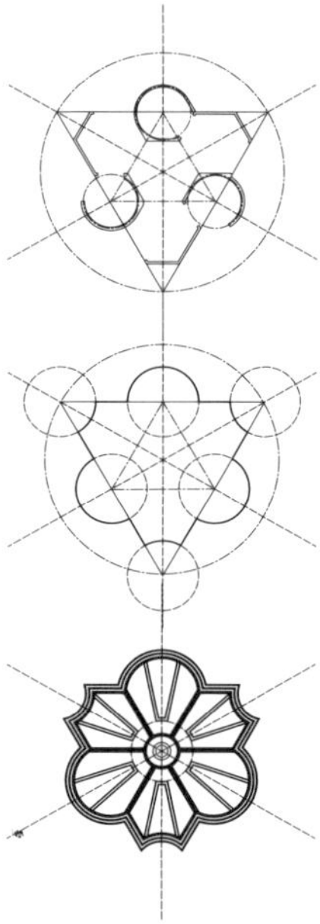

Fig. 10-12: Trefoil geometry comparative study between Casa Trevo and Borromini's 'Sant'ivo alla Sapienza' ceiling dome built in Rome in 1660.

Fig. 13-16: Key changing profiles in plan, from rectilinear to curvilinear transitions, along the height of Column_8.

Erecting Figures

The double-page contact sheet on the next page presents a fixed drone shot that was taken weekly during the construction of the house's cast-in-place concrete structure. It slowly reveals how the irregular building up of concrete elements is being implemented by the adopted system of construction, e.g., wall first, slab second, and how its sequencing challenges the fixed diagrammatic figure of the plan. In its place, a transitional geometry guides the process of its construction along with its evolving figure, as shown from above.

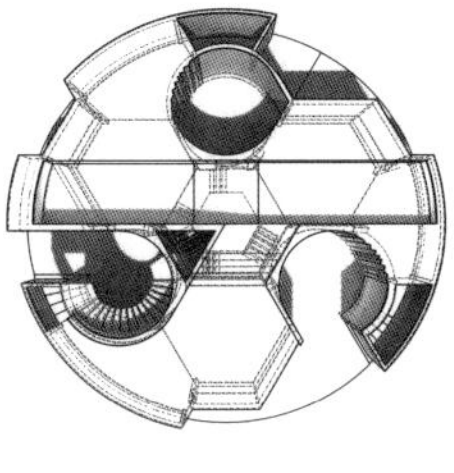

Sky view (from above)

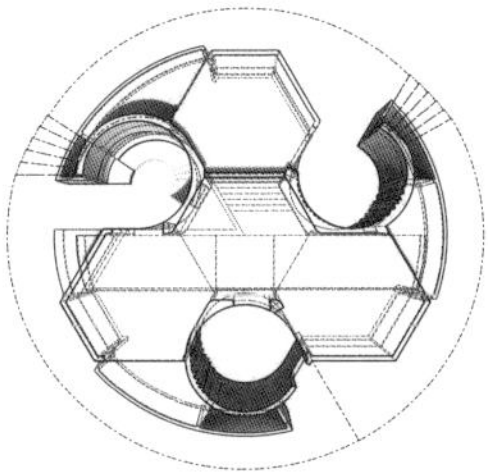

Earth view (from below)

Fig. 17-18: Top and bottom perspectives.

GROUNDED SKY
(on ground: response to site)

One of the design intents was to raise ground as roof and insert the space of the house under it, while keeping the terrain as untouched and natural as possible. By elevating the ground plane to the roof datum, a latent space is left open beneath for an exploration in section to take place. A duality between literal and conceptual ground establishes a first hierarchy between horizontality and verticality, where the sectional outcomes inform any final demarcation in plan. The literal ground has one side; a ground slab impacting the soil with some of its area excavated below grade. In contrast, the conceptual ground is double-sided; roof and ceiling impress on the space above and below, articulating a new kind of deep façade for the project; an embossed plate facing the sky.

Cast on Earth

A past project experimenting with the construction sequence of raising a ground slab to a roof datum was Earth Formwork. Conceived as a prototype for an open-air community centre in rural Botswana, the proposed procedure was as follows:

Step 1) Cast on earth: modulation of the soil to perform as formwork for the concreting of a foundation slab. Step 2) Cast on cast: duplication of the foundation slab by casting, in parts, a second slab on top of the original. Step 3) Formwork reversed decentring: three steel hollow columns are fixed to help hoist the new ground slab into posi-

Fig. 19: From start (top left corner) to finish (bottom right corner on opposite page), the contact sheet is read horizontally by rows across the two pages.

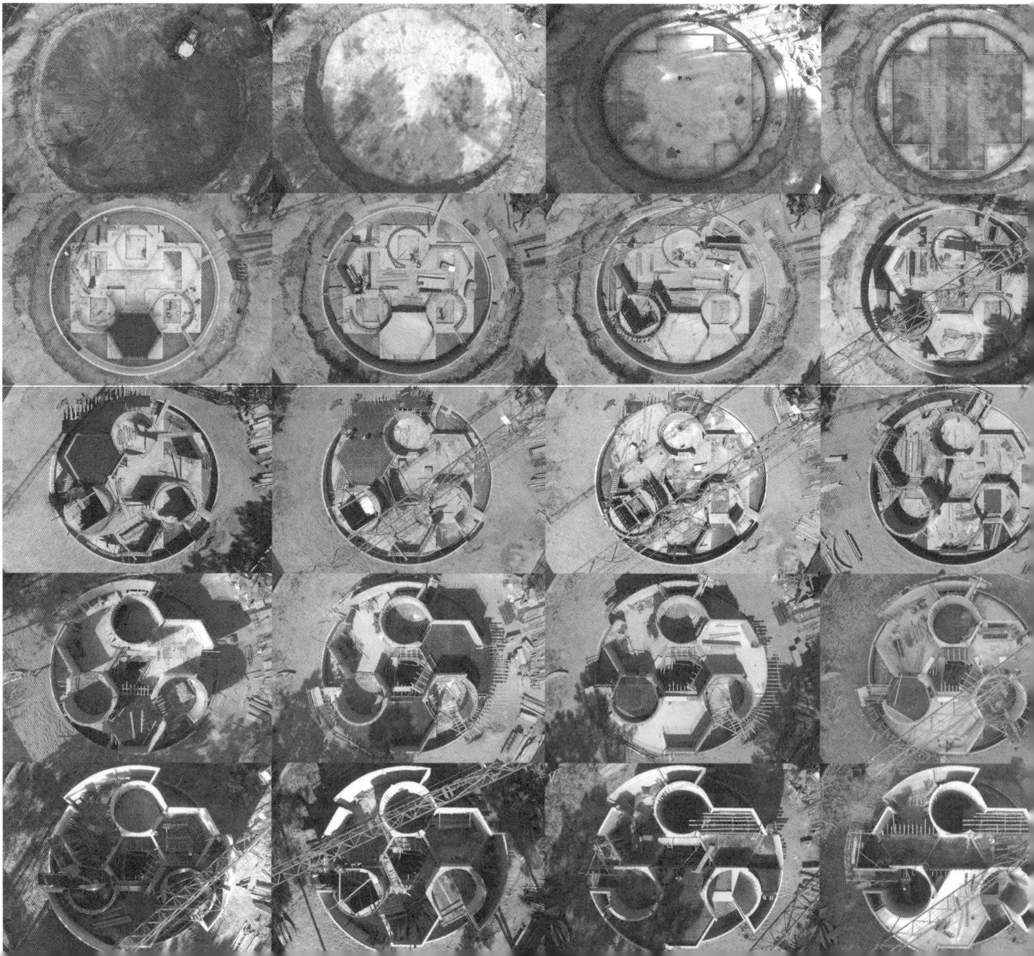

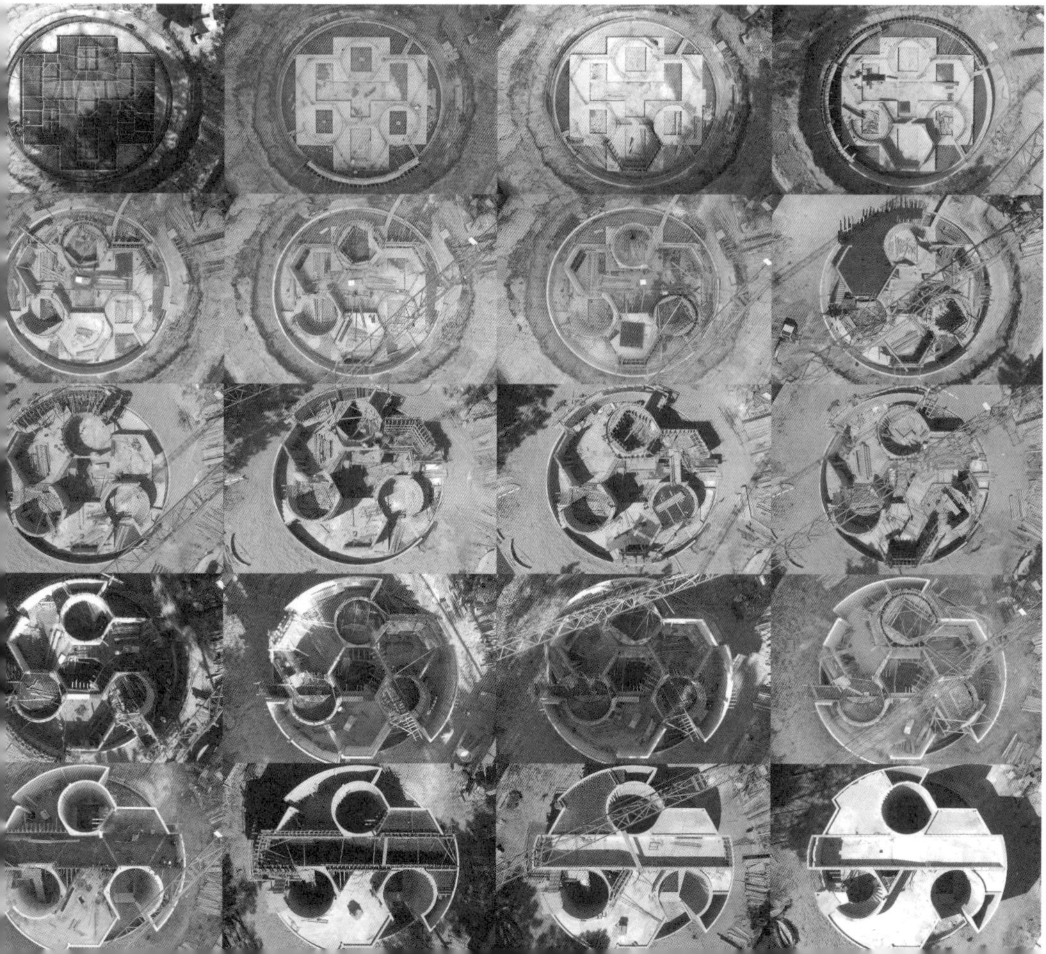

tion, establishing a new roof datum that reveals the accentuated impression of its ceiling.

The spatial character that emerged from this prototyping experiment was mostly conditioned by physical forces; that is, by the tension and compression captured between the impacted ground and the embossed ceiling of each partial slab. In that regard, the prototype is procedural and not form-driven. The pronounced form would only derive from working closely with the unique properties of modeling soil as means of formwork. Although this procedure only went as far as a general concept for the building, like other developmental projects it remains inside a toolbox of ideas still germane to future applications. New projects never really start from nothing, but mainly originate from the transformation of precedent prototypes. The implementation of a similar construction system for the house was quickly abandoned and not literally applied, due to differences of economy, culture, size of project, building permission and risk assessment. However, the main concept was to elevate ground on three hollow columns, operating almost like jacks, to a new conceptual datum, while maintaining the initial hypothesis to test the design exploration of an alternative organisation of space; that is, free from any horizontal impositions of a slab to wall to slab hierarchy, and not least (re-) invigorated by the laws of gravity.

Fig. 20, 21: Diagrams of construction procedure demonstrating the design method.

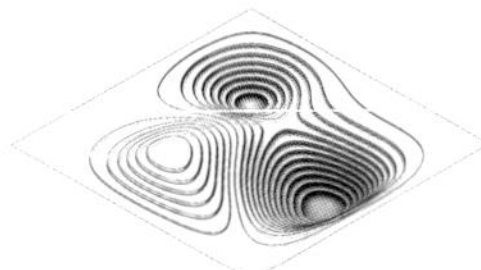

Fig. 22, 23: Photo of model conveying the main spatial idea of the prototype and the original ground excavation for earth casting.

Literal Ground (recto)

In the work, gravity is considered to be an amplifier of an experience of space; a positive force relating to weight and volume, from which space exudes a potential tension and/or compression. For instance, the way the house sits or is anchored to the ground presents a first design opportunity exploiting this gravitational intent. There is a topographical difference of more than 1m within the footprint of the house. The excavation and foundation work take advantage of this site characteristic by stepping the ground slab into two levels and pressing the overall mass of the house lower in some areas than normally expected. A changing pressure on the soil can be witnessed as its periphery gradually rises above, i.e., the terrace slab is flush with grade on the south side and sinks below grade on the west side where the earth is held in place by an exposed retaining wall.

Fig. 24: Top view of excavation and finished structure.

This concrete mass impression on the excavated earth and its subsequent level difference of spaces, also acts internally as a springboard from which the vertical circulation begins pushing upwards to reach the raised living-room datum. Outside, two external staircases, located east and west, mediate the main level difference. The transition between these two heights alters the subject's perception of scale in relation to varying degrees of proximity to the hovering mass above, whose main elements also shift in size, in relation to the site's level difference. A 1m topographical change seems negligible and the excavation work could have simply flattened it at an extra cost. Instead, it is fully exploited for what is about to emerge in the articulation of the spaces above.

Conceptual Ground (recto-verso)

By virtue of being conceptually unearthed and physically uprooted, the roof's double-sidedness is not only revealed but used as a device to accentuate the sense of weight pressing down on the various rooms below and to generate volumetric differentiations. Its main feature is a 20m long lap pool of varying depth (from 1.2 to 2m water clearance), oriented east-west and spanning the entire length of the house: it is the metric ruler of the house. The beam of water cuts through a series of spaces below, differentiating their ceiling heights, e.g., in the bedrooms, bathrooms, and atrium, while cantilevering out on both extremities.

The perception of the irregular three-dimensional ceiling is experienced as if one is located in the earth itself looking up; a kind of partial archeological earth view of the house's underbelly. On the flip side, the rooftop is experienced as a release or distancing from the internal logic below; a sky view at 9m altitude. A split in level, echoing the topographical difference at grade, anchors two main terraces, each capping the roof. The lower one is accessible via a spiral staircase running up the face of one of the adjacent outdoor patios. Upon entering the main roof terrace, one still needs to cross over the open void of a bathroom skylight. The concealed bathroom skylights are also groundless, acting as a visual frame to one of the external ground stairs at grade. This moment of vertigo is a last reminder of the house's sense of verticality, sandwiched between two grounds, before one finally enters a more secluded and serene environment. From the lower terrace, five more steps lead to the pool, level with the upper part of the terrace on the opposite side and mirroring the sky on its water surface.

Fig. 25: View along the belly of swimming pool, pressing down on the spaces underneath the roof terrace.

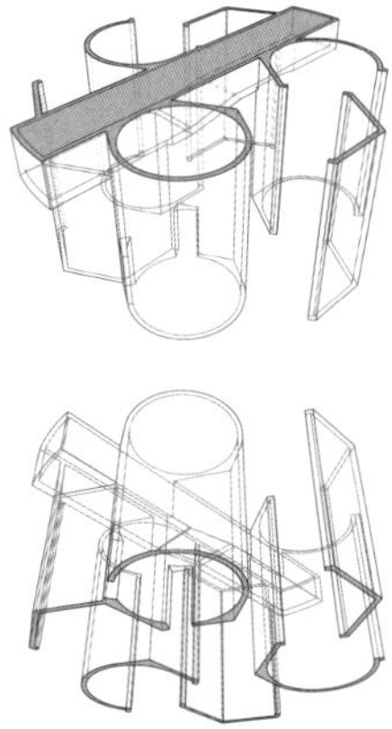

Fig. 26: Views of principal vertical structure holding a cantilevered beam of water.

VOIDED STRUCTURE
(on structure: vertical)

The structural imperative caused by lifting the ground towards the sky prompts an ensuing architectural idea for the house; the potential for an added experience of space provided by the inhabitation of its main structure, material and resulting forces. To this effect, three sizeable primal elements are introduced to support a newly defined roof-scape. This tripartite arrangement asserts the vertical axis as the major structural element, consequently liberating the slab. The provision of these hollow and spatial columns supports a roof slab and an oversized beam, while they also perform as outdoor patios. These semi-open shafts offer a first spatial ambiguity between inside and outside boundaries. They also accentuate a vertical scalar displacement, causing a differentiated sense of gravity between elements; a proposition for structure to additionally perform as pure habitable space.

Hollowed Out

The premise of a semi-open and voided column as an active architecture element for the house

. 27: North-south section showing the various rooms and ide-outside relationships.

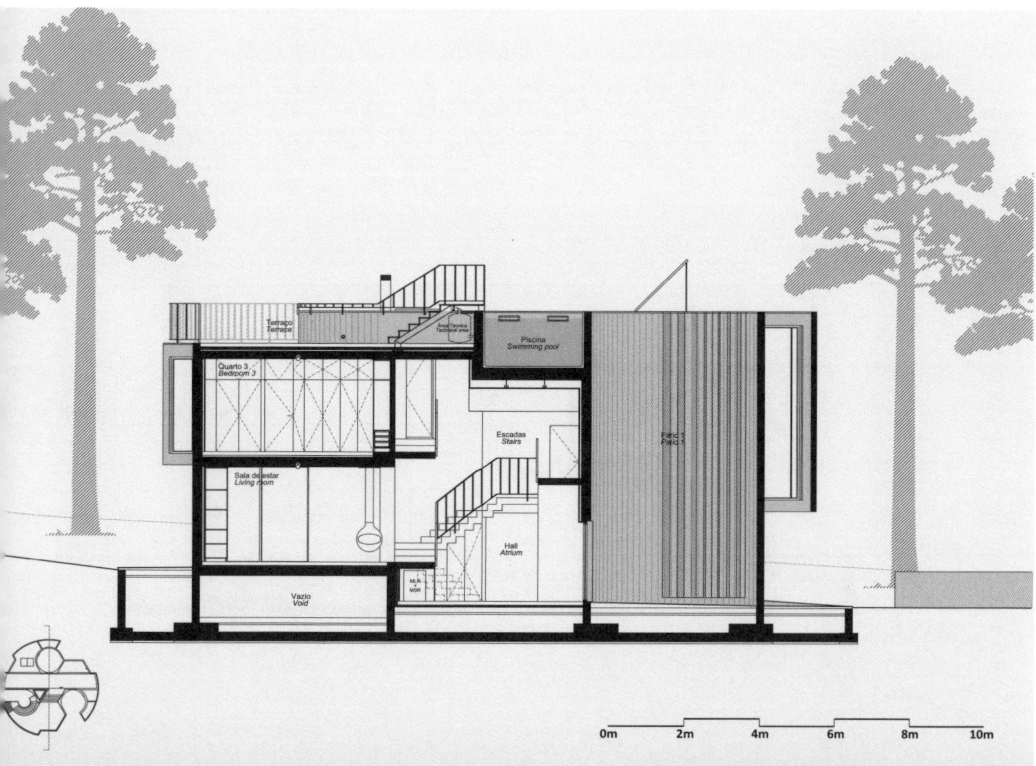

Fig. 28: East-west section showing the various rooms and inside-outside relationships.

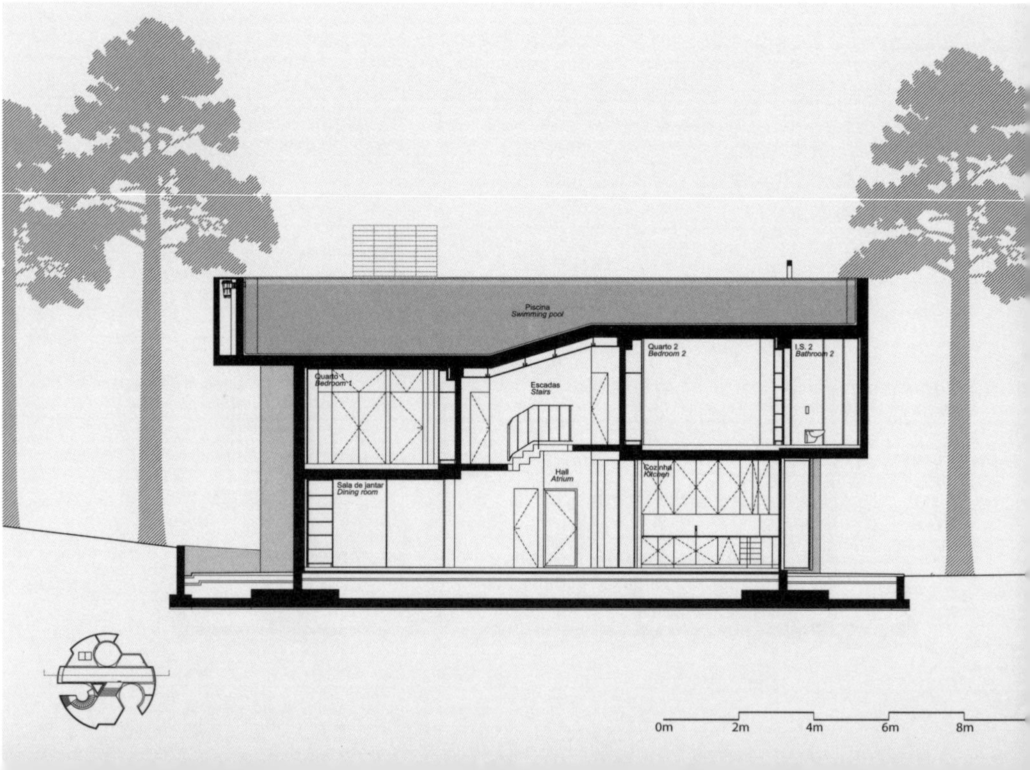

29: North-south section showing the various rooms and de-outside relationships.

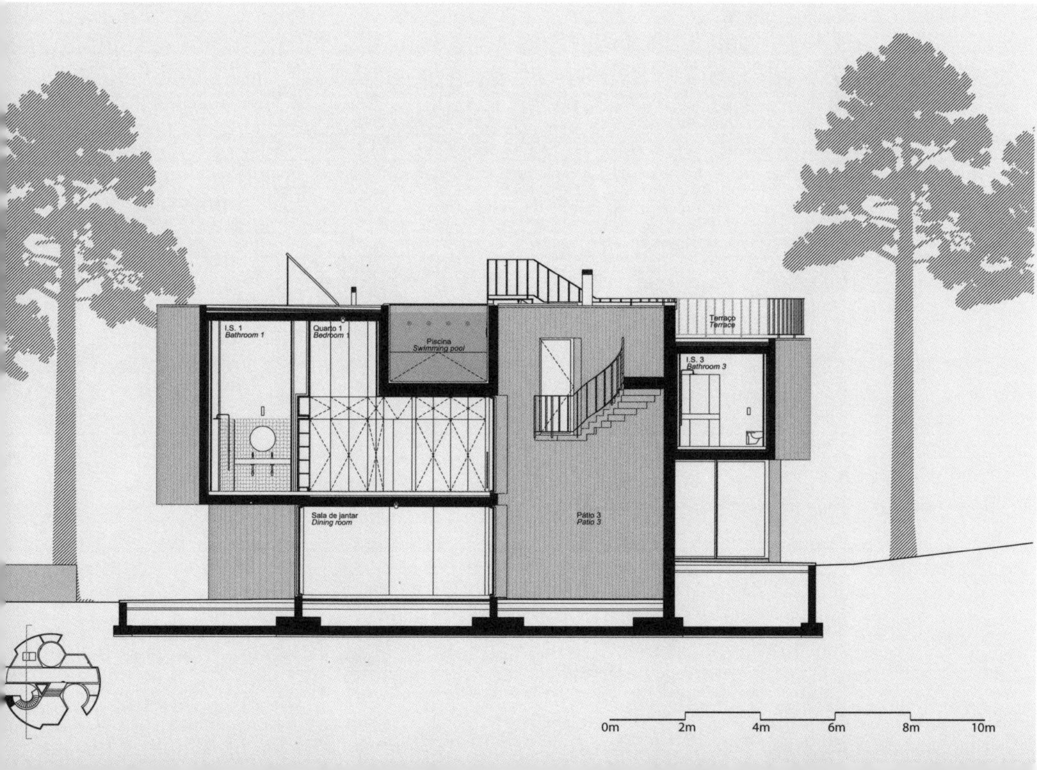

Fig. 30: Swimming pool seen as void during construction.

originated from the making of column_4 of New Orders. At the column scale, it proposes a hollowed out vertical shaft with a partially open perimeter. The column extrusion mediates from one type of outline at the bottom to another type at the top, causing a thickness change in plan but also in section. At the scale of a tower, the central inner void becomes an open courtyard for intra-mural living, disclosing an internalised life tuned to its specific environment. A horseshoe figure of 270 degrees finds its opening oriented west to invite in maximum sunlight. Feedback from solar exposure analyses of its inner surface for one calendar year informs the column's changing thickness. In zones exposed to longer and greater sunlight, the thickness increases to provide deep shaded spaces, whereas in more shaded areas, it remains minimal. An averaged yet irregular massing serves as a rough canvass for different types of living to take charge at another operative scale; through the further concrete articulation of its inner surface by means of undercutting channels inwards.

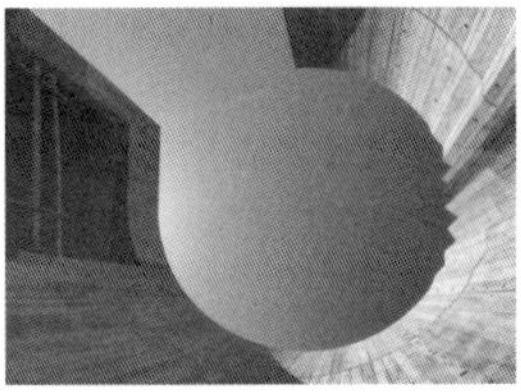

Fig. 31, 32: Top and bottom views of one of the house's hollow columns: It performs as structure, patio space and lightwell. The architecture element was directly borrowed and transformed from column_4 of New Orders.

Pocketed Space

Subsequently, column_8 of the same project experiments with a series of deep-shaded or recessed spaces, defining both their interior and exterior perimeters by virtue of being porous. Organised in stacked sections, a sequence of different profiles investigates various degrees of openness along the vertical axis of the column. In order to maintain the legibility of its overall extrusion and more continuous transitions, the interpolation of curvilinear surfaces between each different profile is geometrically rule-based, i.e., made of rotating straight lines. The geometrical rationale is described by the irregular movement of a straight line over time. It enables their easy translation into formwork made of straight timber elements, even though the forms are highly pronounced three-dimensionally. This idea of tectonic introversion through recessing voids into the mass of column_8 was also extracted and put to full use in the articulation of the house patios

Fig. 33: Introverted space of column_4, and thickness articulation study based on solar analysis.

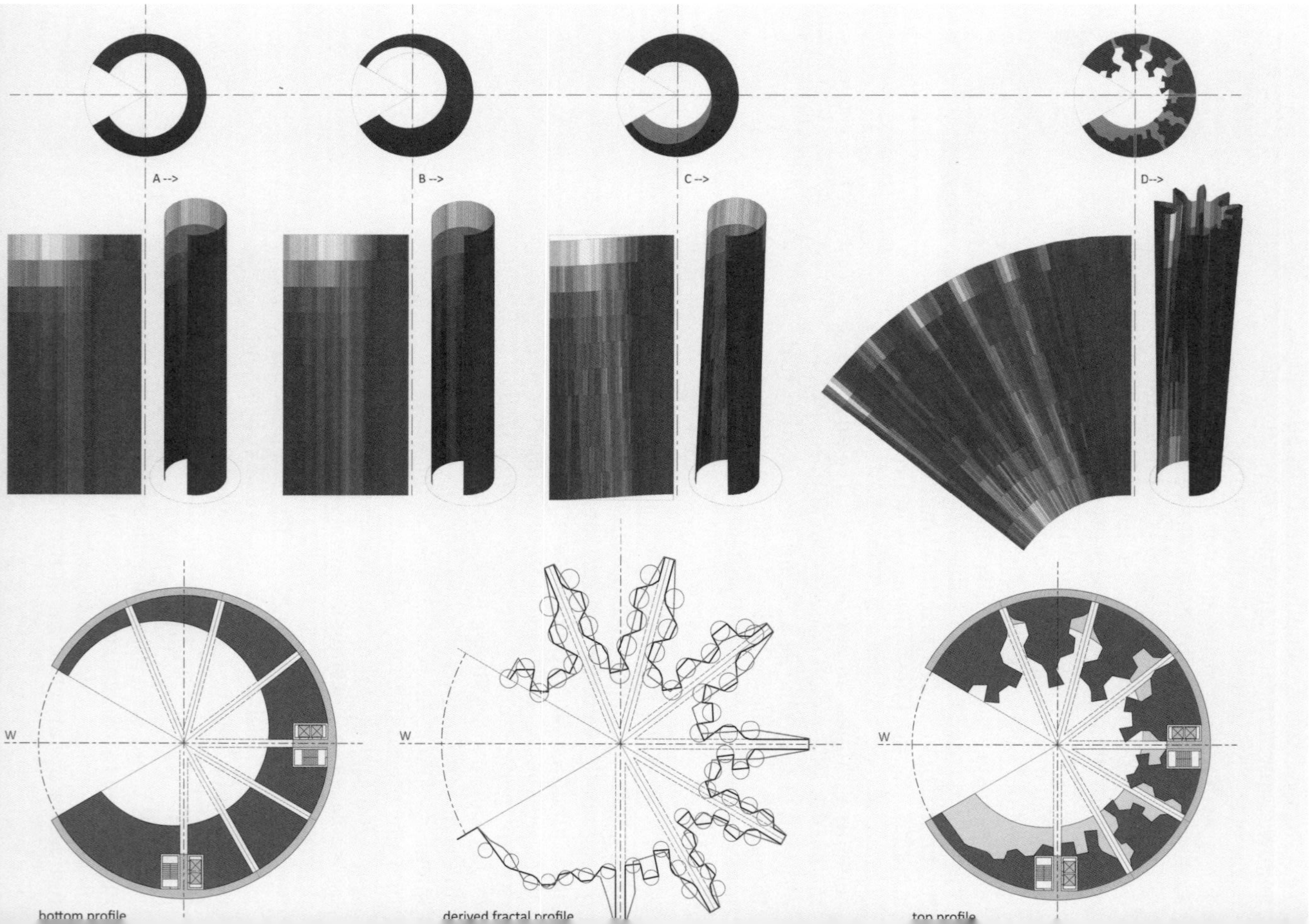

vis-à-vis the house's internal space. They also screen off the various open rooms from their direct outside context.

Three is the Number

The three circular columns, with a diameter of 4.5m and height of 9m each (1:2 in proportion), set up a tripod condition that is not a binary symmetry, e.g., mirrored along only one axis. The choice of three instead of two or four hollow supports stimulates a more eccentric, disorienting and open-ended type of occupation in and around the patios, while excluding more static square spaces. It is worth noting that tripartite relations are often used in the work with various levels of influence as a means to also trigger an imbalance between part-to-whole relationships. There is both a hierarchy of elements in the house and a synthesis of them. The drums play a high degree of importance in that hierarchy; they are the engines and spatial activators of the project.

Structurally, they are primal, in holding the slabs, the rooftop and pool by virtue of overlapping tangentially with the two side walls of the pool. They are void meeting void as first act of structural occupation. The interior space of the house finds its way around them, almost as residual, as a last resort in incorporating a functional and livable space. The patios are expansions of the inside, one being fully enclosed and the other twosemi-open. Extensive in plan, they are identical in shape and area. Their scale in height is monumental compared to other types of volumes existing in the project. They remain fully integrated voids in regards to the overall mass of the house, while structurally holding it up above ground.

Light Shafts

The hollow shafts also present a blank canvass for light, day and night, to become the protagonist animating the life cycle of the house through seasonal changes. Identical in size yet oriented in different cardinal positions, e.g., north, east and

Fig. 34, 35: Views from kitchen and bedroom looking out into the patio spaces. Much sunlight penetrates but views to the site are partially blocked, giving a sense of privacy and introversion to the interior spaces created.

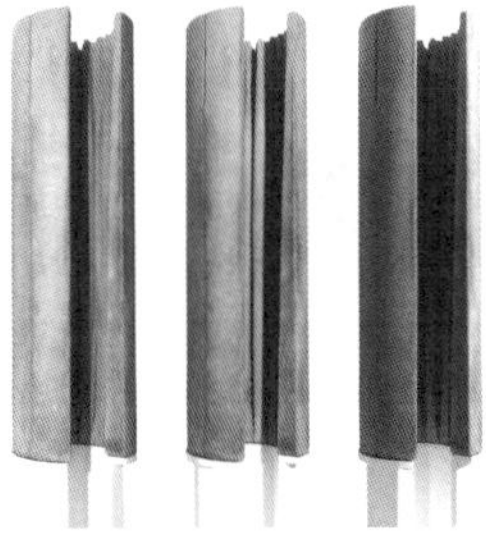

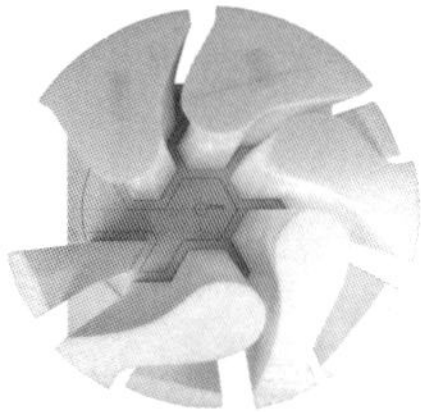

Fig. 36, 37: Recessed profile spaces of column_4 and formwork prototyping of changing extrusions of column_8.

west patio, they each internally and externally illuminate the spaces of the house in very specific ways. Zones of solar exposure descend and ascend the depth of each patio throughout the day, in stretches of time overlapping from patio to patio. A particular light quality tuned with time emerges. It begins in the east in the morning, illuminating the kitchen and dining areas, reaches its brashest moment at midday, and attenuates westward as the afternoon passes, slowly dimming the light in the living quarters of the house. There is an intentional play or duality between the evenness of the object, passive at times, and its animated variability rendered from contextual media such as sunlight. This alone already does plenty to produce the heterogeneity sought by the project. (The passage of light in the patios over time is further explained later in the Curtained Wall section.)

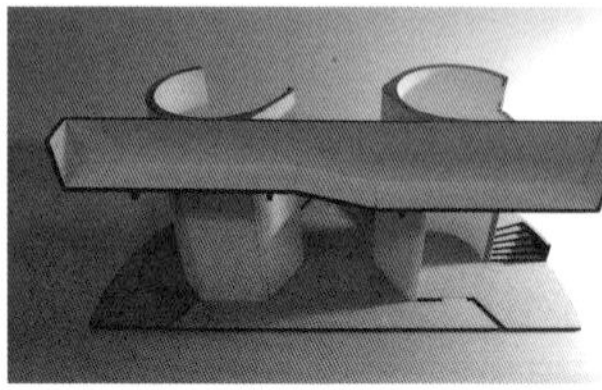

Fig. 38, 39: Sectional process model showing the initial structural setup with hollow columns holding the pool, and complete model with three hollow columns as structural tripod.

SHATTERED SLAB
(on slab: horizontal)

As walls come first, floor slabs are made second, and are therefore independent from their traditional and rigid building sequence: slab, wall, slab, etc. Disintegrated into bits that are more attuned to their specific room sizes, the dominance of the horizontal datum has at last made way for a variety of volumetric spaces. Each partial slab gradually pushes up against the irregular ceiling plane of its embossed roof slab to render each room unique in section, albeit similar in plan. Ascending around the central shaft of the hollow atrium, the circulatory path linking each height datum provides a large degree of fluidity in movement, in return creating the ascending spatial experience of the house to become all but static; a vertical release from the fixed plan.

Core Circulation

This is an opportune moment to expand more on the circulatory strategy and its relation to the spatial sequence. The house is formally accessed through a solid door on the northern patio, which

40: Link between circulation and blown up slab.

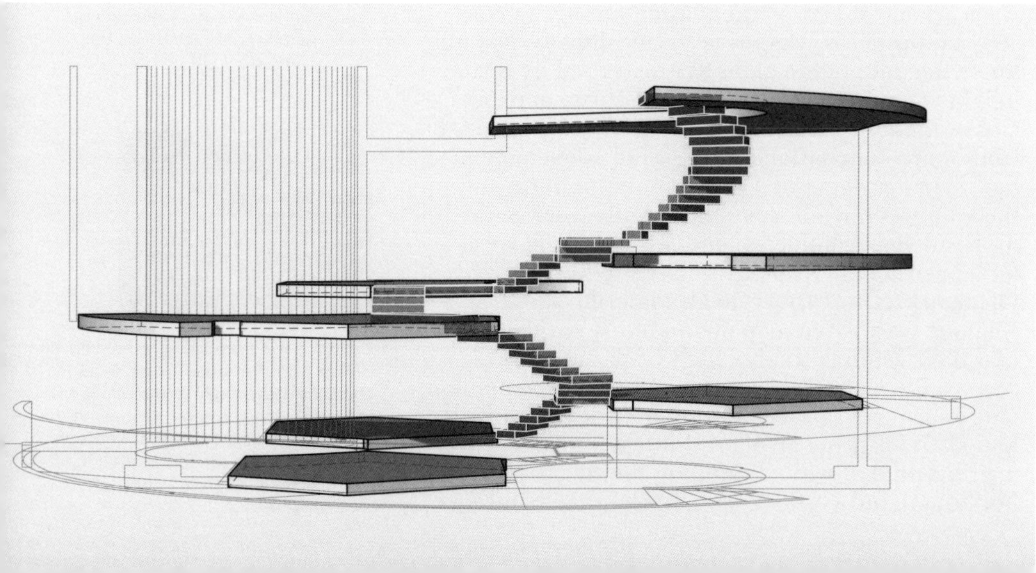

is the only patio completely enclosed in plan, yet designed as a 9m high open sky chamber. Upon entering, one finds oneself still outside. A second glazed door within the patio brings you inside the central atrium, all the way above which is a small triangular skylight, e.g., conceptual key stone, lighting the deep chamber from above. The penetrating light reinforces the underbelly of the swimming pool as part of the protruding ceiling. From the atrium a trefoil space, comprised of kitchen, living and dining areas spreads out between each of the three patios. The kitchen and dining spaces are located at grade, whereas to access the living room, one needs to begin to ascend the house by 1m via the main concrete staircase circling the atrium space. Up above, the stair distributes each of the three bedrooms-bathrooms, located at different height data. This results in different ceiling heights for each room on the first and second floor. Although identical in plan, all spaces are radically different in section and volume. They progressively compress as you ascend the house, room by room, causing a spatial tension and compression from below and above respectively, to demarcate an idea for volumetric living.

Fig. 41: View from second bedroom, showing on the left the stair serving the third bedroom, then leading to the access door of the west patio, where an outdoor spiral stair serves the roof terrace. On the right, the sloping underbelly of the swimming pool above presses down on the atrium space beneath to differentiate two partial height changes in bedrooms one and two.

Fig. 42: View from third bedroom, showing the swimming pool profile in the middle, bedroom two down on the left, and further below the pool, bedroom one on the right. The light from above enters through the triangular skylight located on the rooftop, and the light on the right from the east patio.

Scarred Face

A surprising aspect that emerged out of the construction process was the way the slabs were built. Since the data of the slabs are scattered at various heights and out of phase with the three pouring cycles of the house structure, an alternative strategy, from more conventional systems of construction, had to be implemented to create monolithic junctions between walls and slabs. Walls were built first and steel reinforcements for the slabs were temporarily bent into position inside the walls' formworks. Once concreted and cured, these wall sections were later reopened, almost surgically, and their reinforcements bent back outwards to receive the slabs' formworks and reinforcements and to provide proper binding between both wall and slab, ensuring structural integrity. This rather unconventional way of building hierarchy between horizontal and vertical elements supports the

Fig. 43: View from living room, showing on the right the kitchen space below; in the middle the entry to the house from the north patio outside; on the left the stairs ascending to the first bedroom; and on the right again, the stair landing to the second bedroom above the kitchen.

44: Axonometric view of circulation with slabs distribution on top and with volumetric chamber below.

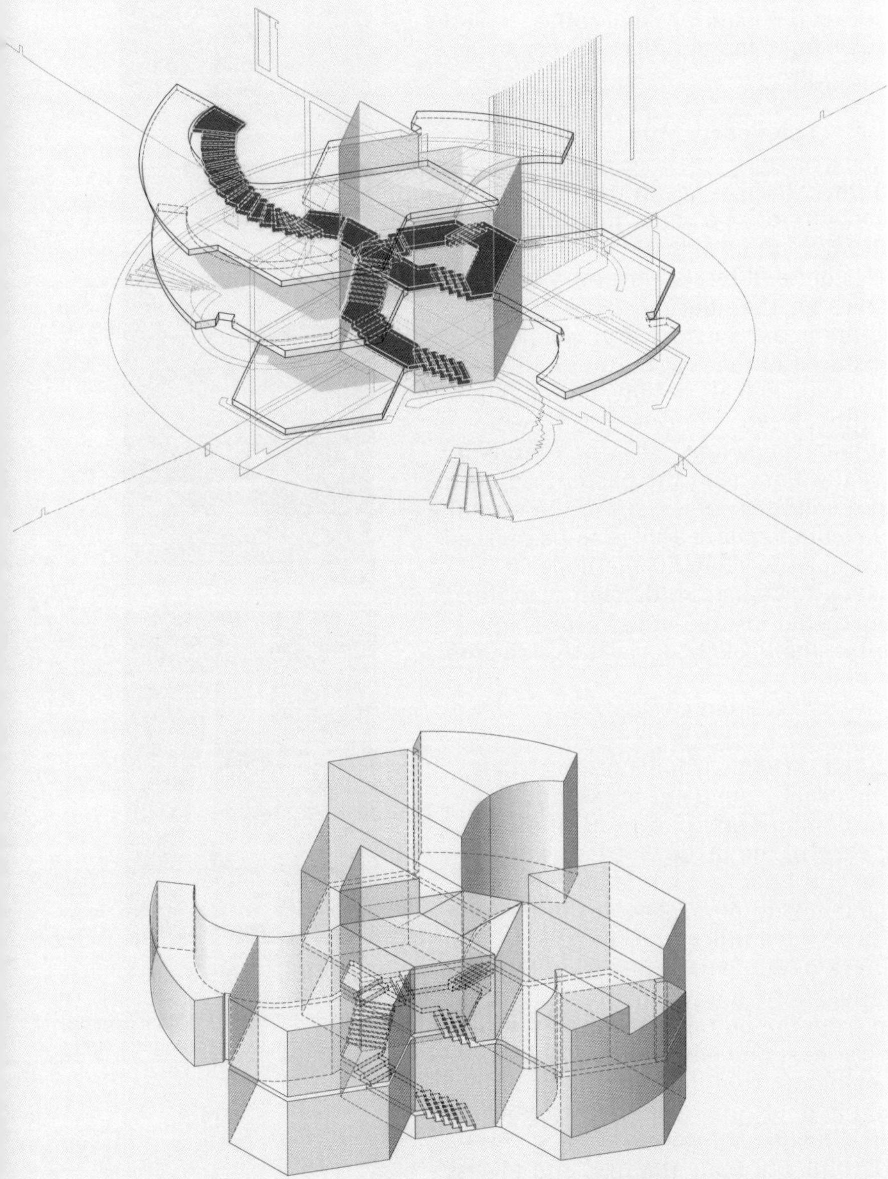

design intent to edit out the dominance of the horizontal datum in the project. In turn, the mass reading of the house on the exterior is also increased by having no perceivable horizontal traces of the slab to be read on the exterior. This rather unique construction system demonstrates how construction follows concept.

The Fourth Void

The central internalised space of the house is also a negative space in its own right, in addition to the three hollow columns or patio spaces. This atrium space is defined by its periphery where all design moves for the house are synthesised at last. While the house's external envelope is precisely registered at the top, bottom and sides, its core internal space feels hollow, undefined, somewhat empty or even church-like; an echo chamber just materialised by what surrounds it programmatically. Porous at the base by adjacent living rooms, it solidifies as it rises to the sleeping quarters and rooftop ceiling above, to be pierced at the top by a narrow skylight; the house's barometer partially depicting the climax of the day, from penetrating beams of light (presented in more detail in the Breached Apertures section later).

Triplets

In examining the three bedrooms more closely, the spatial and scalar impact of breaking the slab is further demonstrated. A precondition was to make each of the three bedrooms the same in shape and area as a common reference to measure changes. In plan, they are differently oriented vis-à-vis each other and therefore subject to different light conditions from their respective patios and window openings; in order of succession from the bottom upwards, they are positioned west, east and south. Their height definition is clamped from both the ascending bottom slabs, the pool volume and rooftop pressing down. Their headroom ranges from 4.5m, to 3m, to 2.5m. At human scale the first and lowest bedroom feels too high and extensive, the second

Fig. 45-47: One of the window types from bedroom one at the bottom, to bedroom two in the middle to bedroom three on the top, showing the scalar change of each in height.

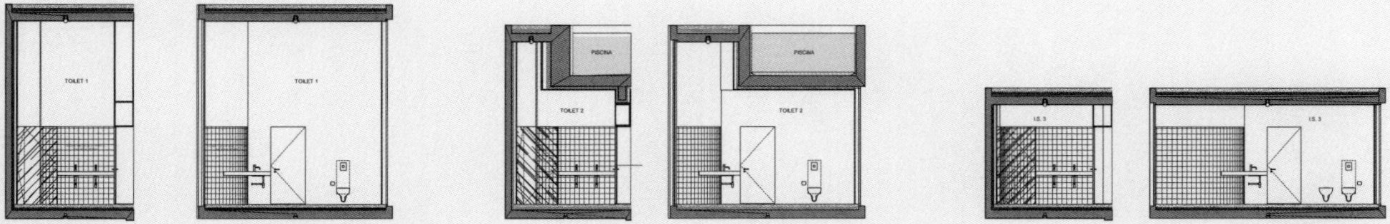

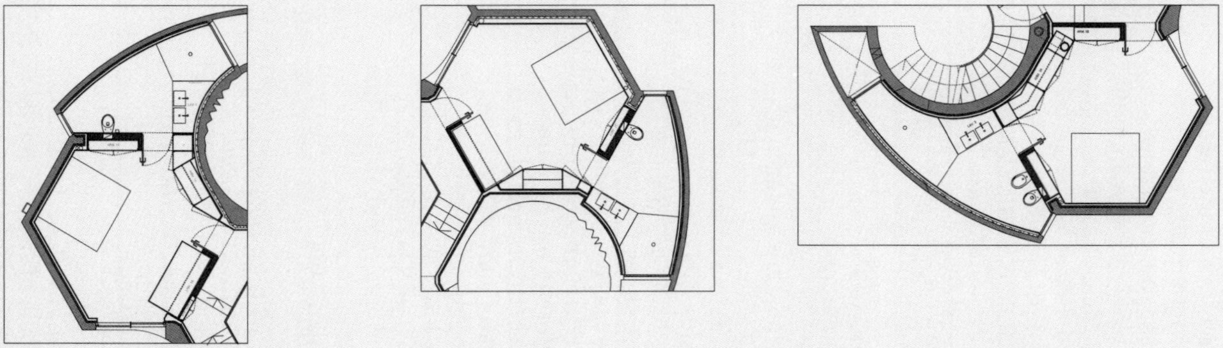

Fig. 48: Cross-sections from bedroom and bathroom one to three, showing their height differences; large, medium and small.
Fig. 49: Identical bedroom and bathroom plans: from left, west bedroom one, east bedroom two and south bedroom three.

almost normal, and the third too low and compressed. What initiated these height changes is the slight topographical difference of the terrain, e.g., 1.08m or six steps, brought inside to trigger a succession of level changes. This is further exacerbated by having the body of the swimming pool cutting through half of the ceiling areas of bedroom one and two, located west and east, to create a secondary level change in those rooms. This elements' intersection further increases a sense of release and compression of space as well as subverting one's reading of scale, e.g., various scales within scales projected out identical plans.

Fig. 50: Shadow projection of surrounding pine trees onto the house's rounded concrete surfaces.

MASKED FAÇADES
(on façade: openings)

The house doesn't take any posture towards its site. There are no privileged vistas, no distant horizon and no strict physical boundaries to address; no front, back or side divisions. In place, it negates its context by vertically addressing its immediate environment. The sky is the site's only vantage point, affirming the rooftop datum as the only façade for the project. This "anti-façades" approach is intentionally reinforced by the house's roundness. As one moves around its periphery, a series of voided intrusions and solid protrusions breaks the circular figure to conceal more of its interior and to exacerbate the lack of clearly defined boundaries in elevation. The envelope is conceived as a cinematic scroll, a filmstrip section where time is rendered elastic and non-chronological with no set beginning or end.

The house is an anti-object with no recognisable façades that can be framed. Instead, it projects one continuous elevation of doings and un-doings of scales, all around its perimeter. At grade, it is relatively porous. From outside, one can, at times, see all the way through the house's interior spaces. Above, large rounded volumes of various heights increase the reading of weight, interrupted at intervals by the tall voids of the slender patio spaces, slicing off vertical chunks of the mass, from top to bottom.

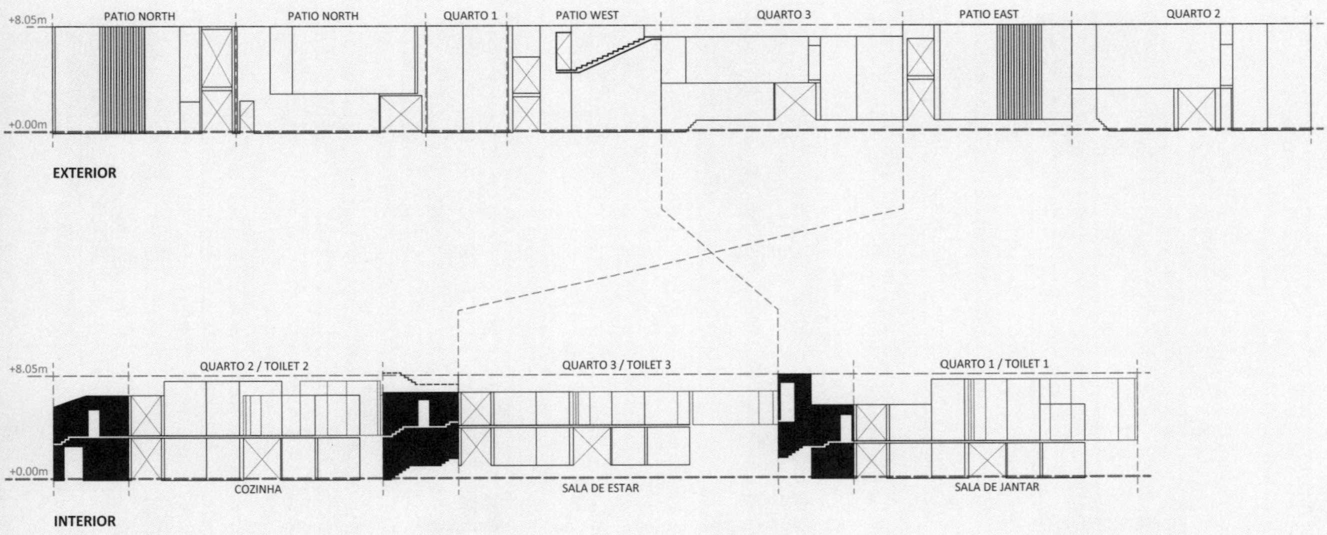

Fig. 51: Unfolded interior and exterior elevations as film reels.

Fig. 52: Selected moments of play of various sized elements around the elevation of the house.

Projected Nature

Surprising effects emerge from the shadows projected onto the house by its immediate natural environment. Not only are surrounding pine trees being cast onto the eastern, western and southern exterior faces of the house, but also, due to the site's proximity to the ocean, a frequent breeze makes these shadows constantly oscillate, liquid-like. The three main circular walls hovering above ground present themselves as protruded screens or blank canvasses onto which a dynamic sense of time is being rendered by these oscillating shadows. This phenomenon reinforces the design intention vis-a-vis the façade(s) of the project. Not only is there a claim that the house has no defined or framed façades to be arrested, i.e., front, sides and back; but the very notion of façade is further negated by having some of the outside mirroring or duplicating its surrounding environment. Depending on sunlight, they absorb the texture of the house's context in the form of a camouflaged anti-object.

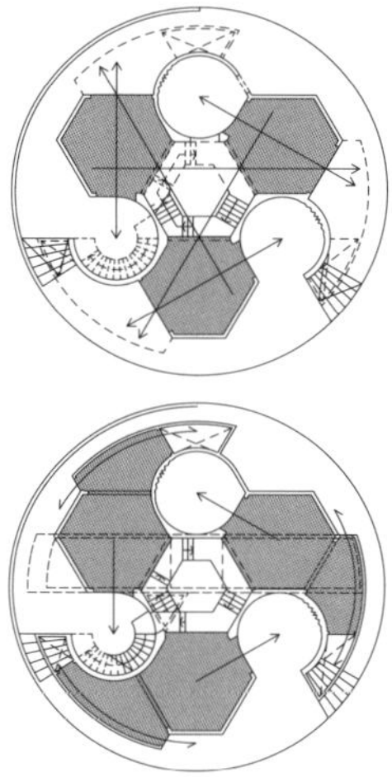

Fig. 53: Diagrams of viewing axes for the two plans conditions of the house: the ground floor is more porous and see-through, whereas the second floor is more introverted towards its site and allows mainly light in.

Breached Apertures

A recurring question when encountering the house from outside for the first time remains, 'Where are the windows?' A house, by connotation, comes with recognisable windows. This one does not. A window often implies a framed feature on the face of an object, a direct perforation releasing views out and inviting light in. The concept of fenestration in this house operates otherwise. Most windows are first concealed from the outside to retain a cohesive reading of the project's mass. There is nothing worth a horizontal view on site. In response, the house constructs its own site internally, breached from place to place by Lisbon's brash light. An inner world is created to be viewed, to view in and through spaces. Its openings only occur as a consequence of specific massing operations; from a displacement between elements, a set of openings emerges. In this regard, the process of generating openings is indirect and comes as a result of design moves with other concerns than puncturing inde-

Fig. 54-55: Above and below the central skylight of the atrium space.

Fig. 56: Studies of external negative volumes for voids subtraction from the house's overall mass.

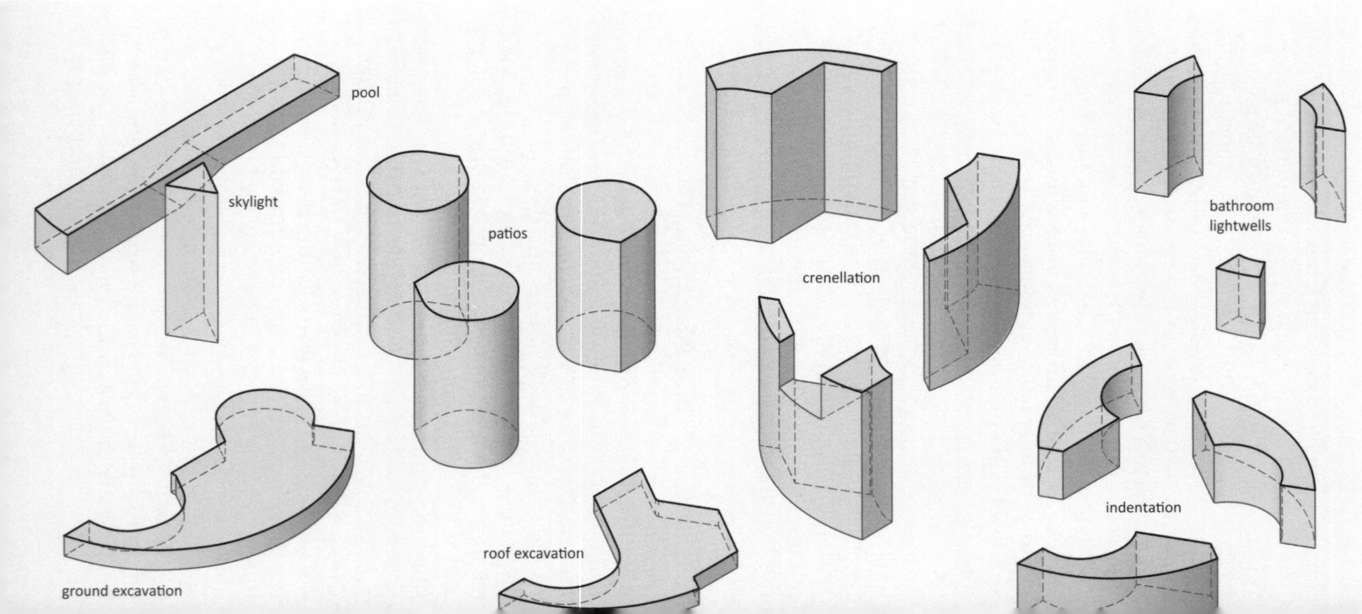

pendent holes into a wall. It is part of an integrated approach to the overall massing of the house. This heading further unfolds various concepts and types of openings for the house relating to different viewing strategies and light infiltrations.

Keystone

Each type of window is repeated three times, identical in plan, different in elevation and orientations. Only the top skylight is singular in kind. Conceptually, it is the keystone of the house, a geometrical void or tolerance demarcated by a three-dimensional gap. From the top view, it is seen as a plain equilateral triangle. Internally, its underside is spatially negotiating height differences between the pool's sloping underbelly, the roof's flat ceiling and one of the patio walls piercing through. It is also marked off-centre from the atrium's main circulation space for external measurement reasons, creating an effect of imbalance inside as one rises up. The lighting effects coming through this small aperture can be characterised by a fast changing and short-lived beam of light, a vector pointing downward and scanning the 9m depth of the central atrium space.

Fig. 57: Play of scales produced by the concrete structure.

Fig. 58: Nine columns-towers from the New Orders project, placed in their intended urban context in Hong Kong, China.

CONTRASTING SCALES
(on scaling up and down: from precedents)

In order to produce scalar shifts in the spatial disposition of the house, elements of different sizes are introduced to its massing. Some are more vertically pronounced, while others are horizontally arranged to form an integrated concrete monolith of multiple notations of scales. Moments of tension and compression emerge as a result, creating, internally and externally, a range of dynamic and varied experiences of space. The intended collisions and overlaps of differently shaped volumetric elements, performing as voids vis-à-vis the overall mass of the house, generate a perpetual doing and un-doing of scales while attempting to read the relative size of the object. Projecting out like a porous stone, the concrete house can never come to rest, otherwise it will become a mere static object, indifferent to site.

Scale is Relative

The question of how big or how small the building is concerns the perception of scale, or rather the illusion of it given by the object. In some areas, the project gives the impression of being monumental, while in other parts, it seems more closely connected to the ground and human scale. This is caused by offering different relational measures between volumes, masses and voids, with their hierarchy shifting either vertically or horizontally, based on one's position in relation to the concrete structure; a subtle doing and undoing of scales, making it difficult to capture everything in one instant. While sizes of elements are predetermined, the perception of scale is relative and therefore visually evasive.

The liberty of scaling masses up and down in the New Orders project did not come without friction or without debates. Yet, the unapologetic approach of prototyping 1:1 scale columns simultaneously with speculative towers for living at 1:100, turned out to generate knowledge that was ultimately productive when it was fully exploited at the scale of a house.

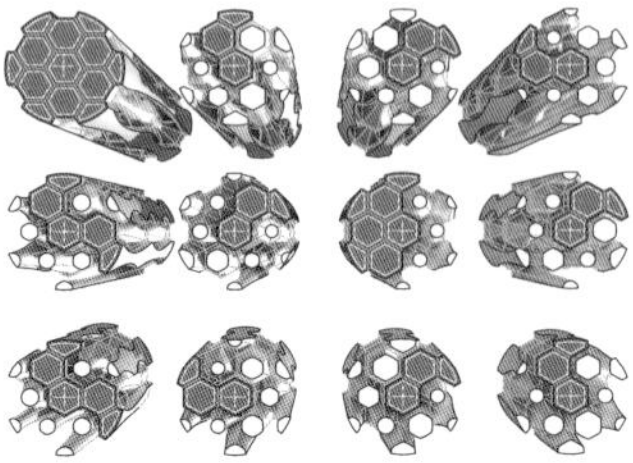

Fig. 59, 60: Plan type studies of column_7 versus inside-outside relationships of spaces in the house, demarcated by its plan figures.

Size versus Scale

Although the project was not conceived that way, subtractive mass studies were conducted to evaluate the robustness of the inter-relations of different sizes of elements in regards to their integration with the overall mass. A taxonomy of voids with different sizes and programmatic roles was identified on the main exterior volume to establish a hierarchy of sizes contrasting with their perception of scales. The same analytical approach was carried out on the interior, to study the contrasted volumetric spaces, even though they are identical in plan.

Three Operative Scales

Three interconnected operational scales were recognized in the design of the house: object, tectonic and detail scales. They each draw from specific

61: Diagrams of exterior voids and interior volumes
tracted from the primitive cylindrical mass of the house.
nitive cylinder with voided internal core and complete house
ılting from subtraction of all voids, internally and externally.

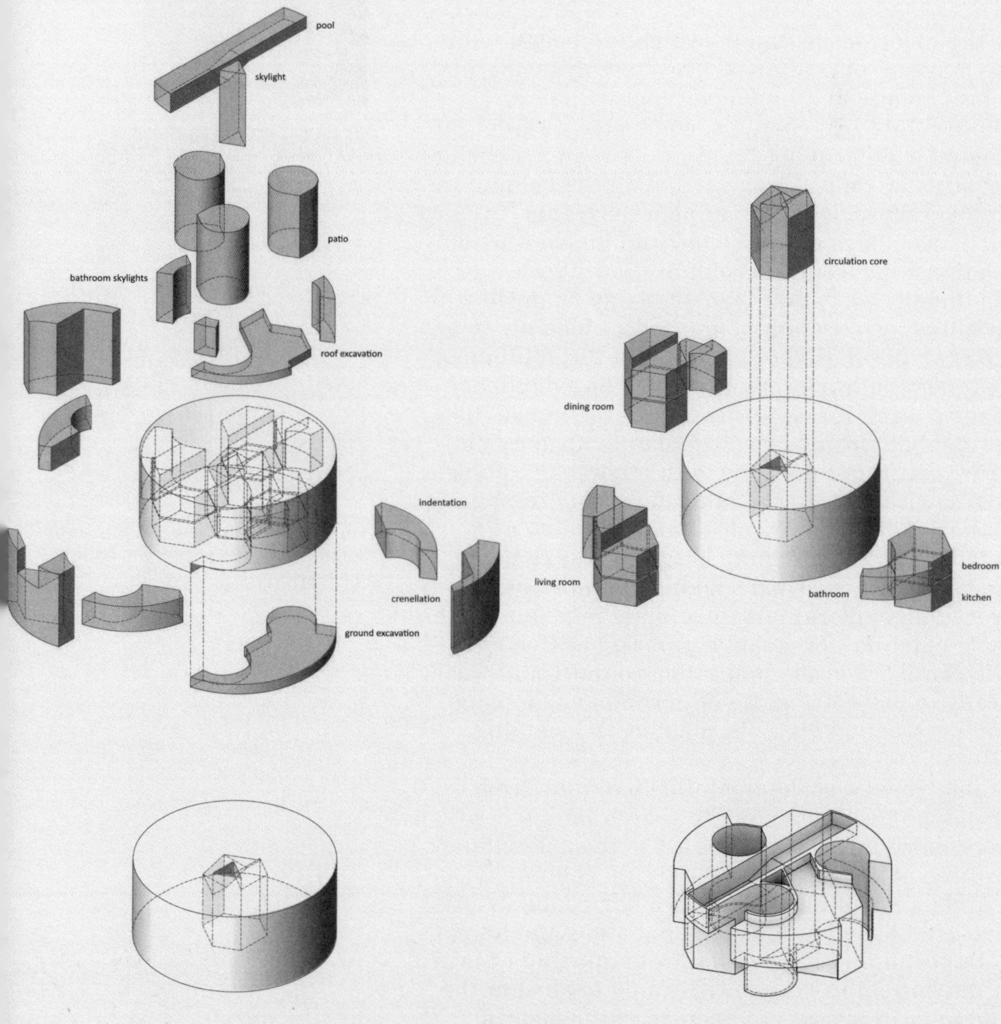

prototyping explorations, conducted before during the New Orders project. Their parallels to and differences from the house's massing, spatial and material characteristics are presented below, and the concurrent design intentions are as follows: to render the space of the house permeable at the object scale; to conceal some of its interiority at the tectonic scale; to amplify its materiality at the detail scale.

At the object scale, the investigation began with the massing of column_7. The column's concrete mass is made of a bundle or aggregation of 13 slender flute-like columns, connected at different heights while leaving room in between for changing sizes of voids. Upon sectioning the column incrementally, a sequence of plan diagrams revealed particular plays of mass-void and inside-outside relationships from the column's periphery. The reading of the column had suddenly changed from an initial aggregation of aperiodic elements to an internal dissolution of the mass of the column. That very characteristic was further extended to the overall massing strategy of the house. Its permeability can be read in plan by incomplete figures, at times merging with others, i.e., polygonal to circular; and at other moments remaining dissociated. The aim is to spatially create a high degree of ambiguity between what's being contained versus what's leaking in and out. The preceding explorations in column_7 facilitated the early potential for a range of massing elements, differentiated in the house horizontally and vertically to project a sense of perpetual expansion and contraction vis-a-vis a subject's location.

At the tectonic scale, the influence came from prototyping column_ 8. The search for spaces that were more inward-looking led to the articulation of three patios in the house. In the column research, a set of four distinctive horizontal profiles was established and distributed along the height of the column. They ranged from opening outward at the bottom to gradually turning inward at the top, to form a series of deep-recessed spaces within the mass of the column. Developable geom-

Fig. 62-63: Deep-recessed spaces of column_8 versus semi-open patios in the house.

etries guided the transition from profile to profile, which disclosed progressively more pronounced undercuts along the column's shaft.

The irregular nature of these extrusions was not followed through in the house design, mainly due to anticipated complexities in formwork construction. Instead, the recessed spaces of the semi-open (in plan) patios were extruded straight. This was enough to bring a visible sense of vertical release internally, while it was externally concealed by holding up massive elements of various heights, e.g., cantilevered pool and bathrooms. In a similar way to the column exploration, the patios retained their erasure character, based on the idea of material subtraction from the overall mass of the project. They primarily perform as 9m-high lightwells, screening large window openings for each living and sleeping room.

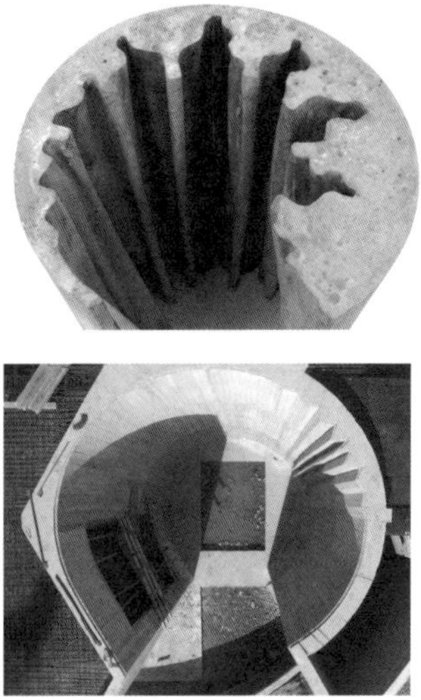

Fig. 64, 65: Concrete corrugation of column_4 versus spatially targeted corrugation inside one of the house patios.

At the detail scale, each patio comprises a blank canvas for something more to take hold over time, and potentially accentuate the materiality of their internalised spaces. To this effect, concrete corrugations are integrated with their patio wall and located in an area of maximum direct sunlight. By incrementally folding in and out of the wall thicknesses, they register various degrees of light penetrations and intensities of cast shadows. The concept of concrete corrugation originated in column_4, experimenting with how natural light can further activate materially amplified surfaces. The column's inner surface was articulated with deep shaded channels running along the column shaft. The more solar exposure it receives in some areas, the deeper the corrugation goes into the mass, in order to provide properly shaded alcoves. The registration of shadow lines into the concrete mass was the concept transferred to the patios of the house. They not only accentuate the vertical reading of each patio, but also emit the impression of an added force into the space. This characteristic is reinforced by having each corrugation suspended from the ground and flush at the top, as if directly coming out of the patios' walls due to material pressure.

These various design intentions, first tested in the New Orders project and later translated to the house, demonstrate how each operational scale and architecture resolution, e.g., object, tectonic and detail, are intertwined to the extent that material and space have become one augmented entity that can no longer be separated, e.g., in the way applied textures can.

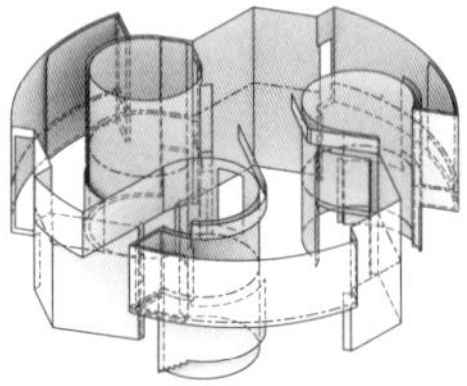

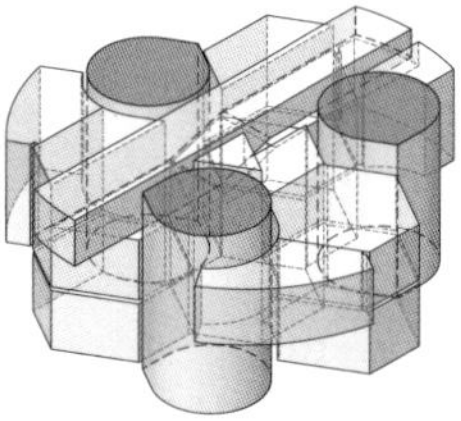

Fig. 66: Drawing analysis of all exposed concrete surfaces versus volumetric study of negative spaces.

Fig. 67: Monolithic concrete structure.

The formal characters of the columns are more pronounced or expressive than in the house, which in comparison may be considered more subdued. The obvious reason lies in the shift from self-built small objects to larger architecture work delegated to contractors. Yet, this is not seen as a loss. On the contrary, that early awareness made the outcome of the house more austere and productively subtle. From an experiential aspect, the house does not express itself all at once. Rather, it is encountered in moments of space and time that are revealed and disappear as the point of focus changes with movement. It is quiet but never at a standstill. It is cold but constantly animated by sunlight. It is monumental in some places but more intimately connected to the ground in others. It is neither planar nor rounded, but a volumetric hybrid. The house is autonomous in the way in which different types of spaces keep changing one's experience of it.

SUPERFICIAL MASS
(on massing: volume)

To render the spatial and scalar concepts active in the house, an important design consideration was to retain the reading of the overall built mass. As little visual interference as possible had to be sustained in order to avoid the breaking down of volumes into disparate planes and surfaces. The detailing strategy adopted was to erase any presence of details or visual breaks that could distract from the perception of a holistic monolith. A cast-in-situ structure is graded by the quality of its exposed concrete. A close scrutiny to formwork design and its proper implementation was essential in the control of its concrete surfaces. This

. 68: Plan drawing of formwork layout of vertical boards: corners are first determined, and then the space in-between illed with some special details using the same formwork hnique.

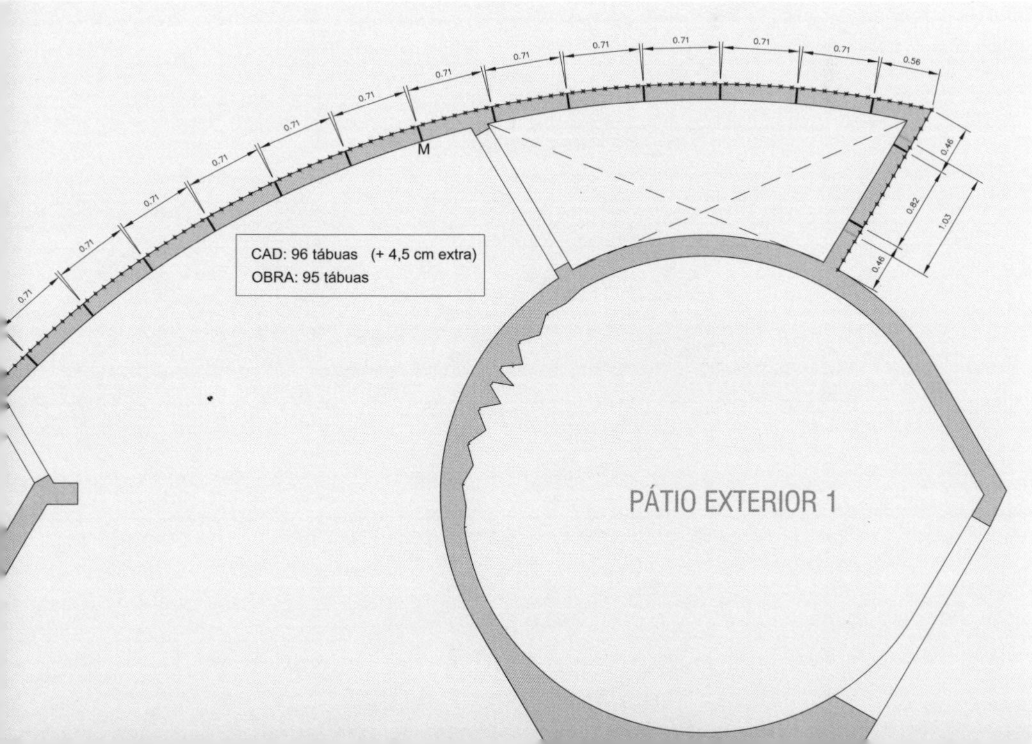

Fig. 69, 70: Layout of even pattern of holes for formwork tie rods in relation to the two horizontal pouring lines. Ceiling plan layout of positions of plywood sheets for formwork construction.

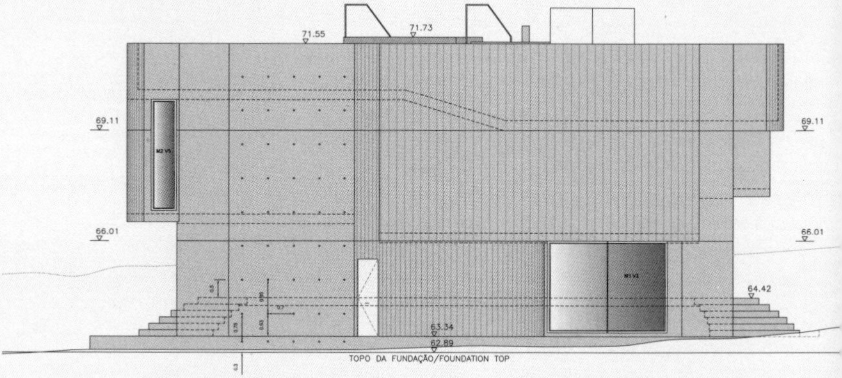

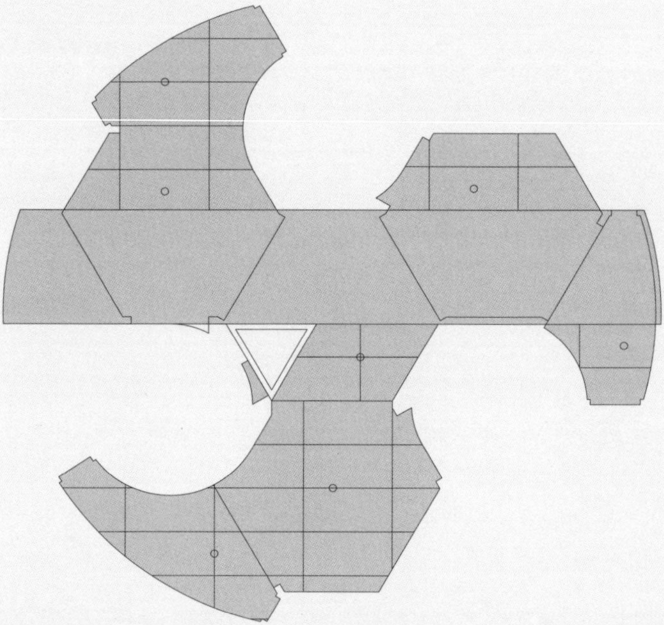

required placing attention, effort and resources on the temporary elements; on the formwork which will eventually vanish while still leaving a trace. The location of these traces vis-à-vis one another becomes crucial if an ambiguity of scales based on continuity and material fluidity between elements is to remain operative in perceiving the mass of the house as one singular entity.

Fig. 71: West view showing resultant mass perception of building from adopted formwork design, animated by light and a combination of natural and geometrical shadow: this view is charged with different types and sizes of volumetric elements but the concrete treatment of surfaces keeps the reading of the overall mass together.

Around the Corner

The focus on formwork was not just about the quality of the surface finishes but more critically about the seamless continuity of concrete surfaces turning corners horizontally, and vertically matching the boards of previous or next pours. To guarantee these smooth transitions, the layout of every single board had to be studied, drawn and accounted for, along with the even distribution of the wall ties across the exposed concrete surfaces. In fact, the metric for the entire house and, by default, its material resolution became the 10cm wide timber board used as formwork for all vertical exposed concrete surfaces on the exterior. Inside the house, only slabs and ceilings remain as exposed concrete, with their formwork layouts also accounted for. The vertical surfaces of the interior walls are plaster boards painted white, over insulated cavity walls, to provide the amount of thermal coefficient required by building codes. The boards' layout of the exterior vertical surfaces begins by detailing each corner's condition, where a concrete plane or surface folds into another one. To guarantee no visual interruptions at these ridges, full-width boards are used at these transitions. The manner in which the surfaces are treated via formwork design becomes the main constructional catalyst to reinforce the mass of the structure. The general detailing philosophy for the house is the erasure of details so that the reading of the mass always comes first.

Fig. 72-74: A drawing, a model at 1:33 scale and a construction at 1:1 scale.

Tailored to Site

In the work, scaled models are representational, whereas prototypes are active experiments with materials regardless of their sizes. Scaled models are used to verify design assumptions, as well as empirical measuring devices, i.e., analogue study of sunlight penetration in the patio spaces, but also as communication tools. A sectional model at scale 1:33 was brought to site for the entire construction of the house to help builders visualise what they were constructing live. Without it, it was too complicated for them, especially at the start of construction, to comprehend the house from drawings only. It was also a very effective medium to discuss architectural details, sometimes drawn on the model directly, and to make quick decisions on site with engineers, contractors and other kinds of sub-contractors.

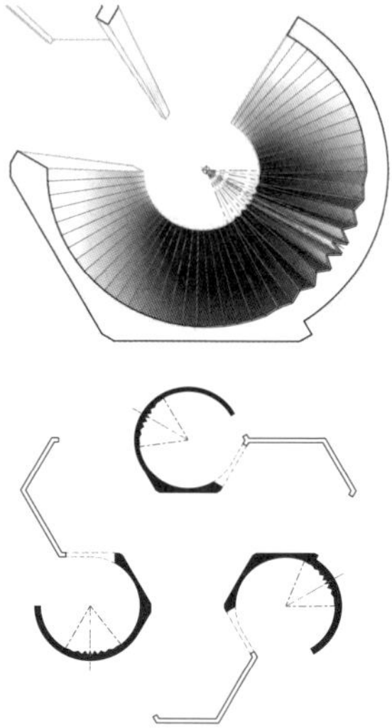

Fig. 75, 76: Type of folded corrugations and their optimal locations inside patio spaces.

CURTAINED WALL
(on wall: detail)

The provision of blank canvasses inside the elemental patios makes room for something more intricate to occur at a detail scale. Progressively folding in and out of the wall thickness of the patios, and calibrated to the specific lighting context, concrete corrugations are made into devices that delay the passage of time through a game of light and shadow. These fluctuating shadow lines extend the vertical reading of the hollow shafts, accentuating a feeling of vertigo and a perception of monumentality. Their gradual incisiveness also pushes the subject away from the patio's inner surface, creating a peculiar sense of resistance within the space of the shaft; a form of pressured space, rendered by void and matter channeling in the mass of the wall and out of the space of the patio. Above all, the physical articulation of these surfaces manifests a life of their own, in tune with its environment as though existing before inhabitation; a time instrument prolonging the autonomy of the house.

Fig. 77: Concrete corrugations experimented across Column_2, 4, 5 and 6 of New Orders.

Evolution of a Detail

A cross-section through preceding projects reveals a recurring interest in a particular concrete character unrestricted to size, technique and

ȷ. 78: Light and shadow projected on the concrete corrugation
the north patio.

function: a ribbon-like effect of weightlessness and fluidity in defiance of the material's current status quo. To begin liquid and end liquid is the ultimate conceptual ambition in working with concrete. It searches for other kinds of solid formations than are otherwise granted by the solid and inert material. Indenting, curtaining, crenellating, undulating, rippling, swelling, bulging, billowing and folding are some of the active surface deviations specific to each of the photos on the right. They portray an effort to stimulate and prolong a heterogeneous sense of fluidity, made possible originally by the liquid state of the material. They undercut mass, as much as pressing it out in irregular ways. Yet, these surface articulations would be short-lived without the complicity of light. Zones of light exposure and shadow cast animate them in aspects that are ever-changing and highly differentiated, rendered at times almost immaterial. The awareness of their responsiveness to light increased as projects evolved from being mainly visual objects at the start to becoming architecture spaces later. Their literal material responsiveness, especially to formwork prototyping, diminished as projects increased in size and complexity with their construction delegated to others.

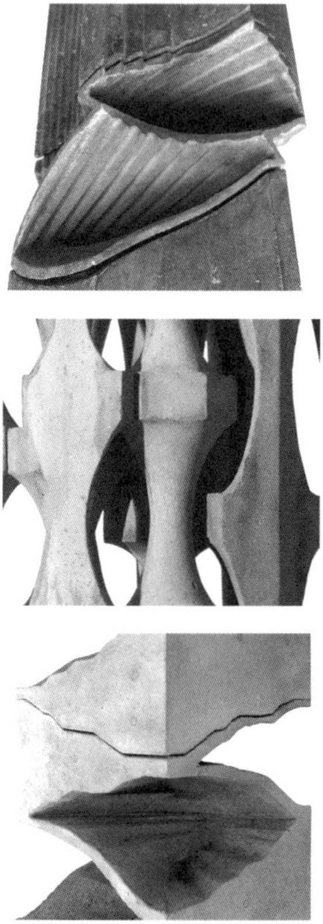

Fig. 79-81: Concrete corrugations experimented across Column_1, 7 and 9 of New Orders.

Light Grinders

Due to the three patios' different cardinal orientations, west, north and east, the amount of direct sunlight they receive from one another varies considerably across a full calendar year. To better understand their interaction with natural light, a series of different light analyses were conducted on each of the three patio spaces. The main issue was to further establish the location of the zones, on the inner surface of each patio, of maximum solar exposure, as well as their time duration and transitions. The intent was to better focus the design and prototyping process of the concrete detail, by specifying the most active zones across seasons in each patio for their material corrugation to maximise the duration of their deep shadow casts and their effect in 'grinding' light. Three

Fig. 82: Analogue sunlight analysis with physical model on site at summer solstice for the three patios: west (top row), north (middle) and east (bottom).

types of empirical methods of different time spans were tested: analogue—surveyed in top view; digital—reviewed in sections; and computational—projected onto unfolded elevations.

Analogue

A sequence of top view photographs was taken, from a physical scaled model of the house brought to site, at each hour of the day when the sun was highest and daylight longest; summer solstice on 21 June. By looking at lighting conditions in the three patios simultaneously, a comparative study of the duration of their overlapping light was made visible. The north patio is enclosed in plan and only top lit, while the other two are both top lit and discontinued in plan: the east patio is open on the south side and the west patio is open on the west side, including a spiral stair climbing mid-air to connect the roof terrace. These tectonic distinctions make their light penetration study harder to grasp. They act as the collective activator of the house's internal space which has many of its openings connected to all three patios. In more direct terms, it is not that one patio's light-well suddenly switches on when the other two are off. Their activity intersects with the outside environment in ways that are less predictable, especially when considering how diffused light bounces off the patio walls and enters through the various openings of the house's interior. Overall, the study showed how each differently orientated patio has its own spatial identity in capturing and emitting light at various time intervals; they function as their own sun clock, as if belonging to three different time zones.

Digital

The second light study was examined in vertical sections, drawn from a digital model. Their viewpoints were taken from each room opening, e.g., living spaces and bedrooms, facing the patio walls directly. This added a visual component to the solar analysis in viewing the patios from inside the house. The timeframe of the one-day summer

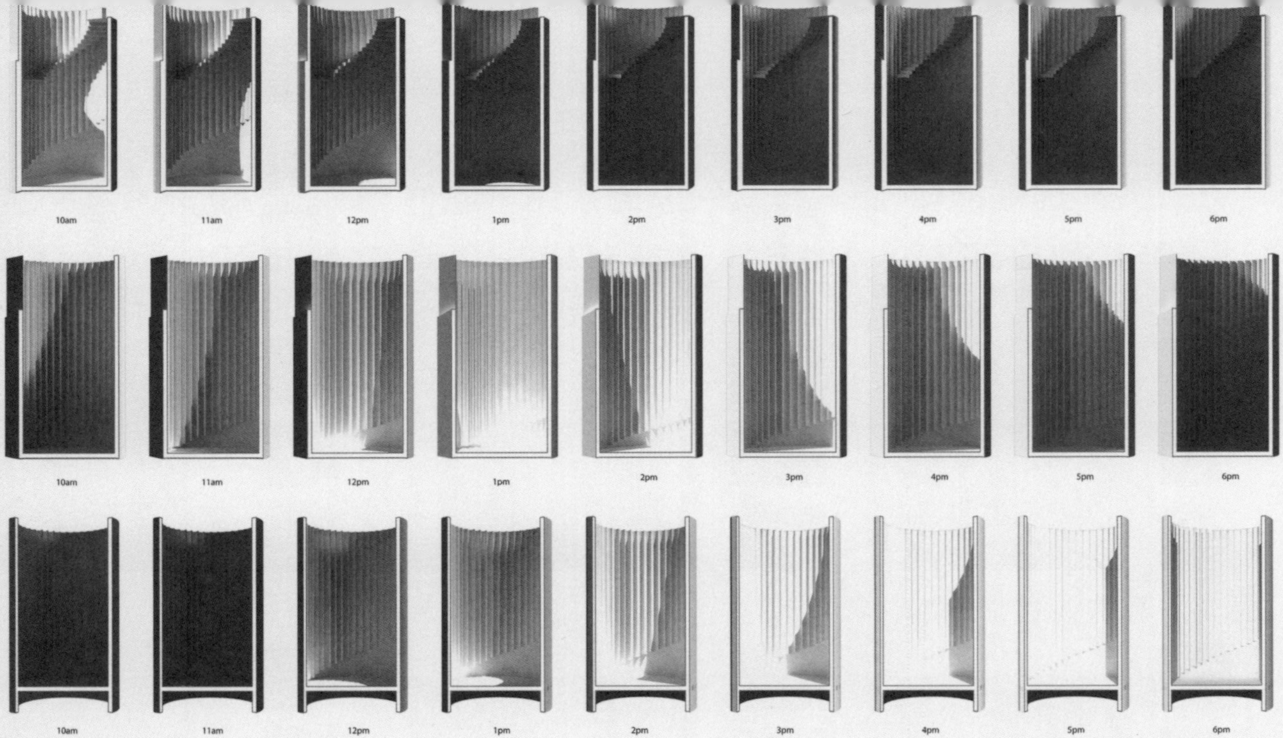

Fig. 83: Shadow analysis for each patio space (west in row above, north at middle and east below) taken in hour intervals during summer solstice (21st of June).

Fig. 84: Solar radiation analyses on inner surfaces of three unfolded patios for a one-year period: equinox, summer and winter solstice. Each main map is an average of a full day solar radiation, from intense to least radiation. The sub-maps are moments of solar radiation taken at morning, midday and afternoon for each of the same days.

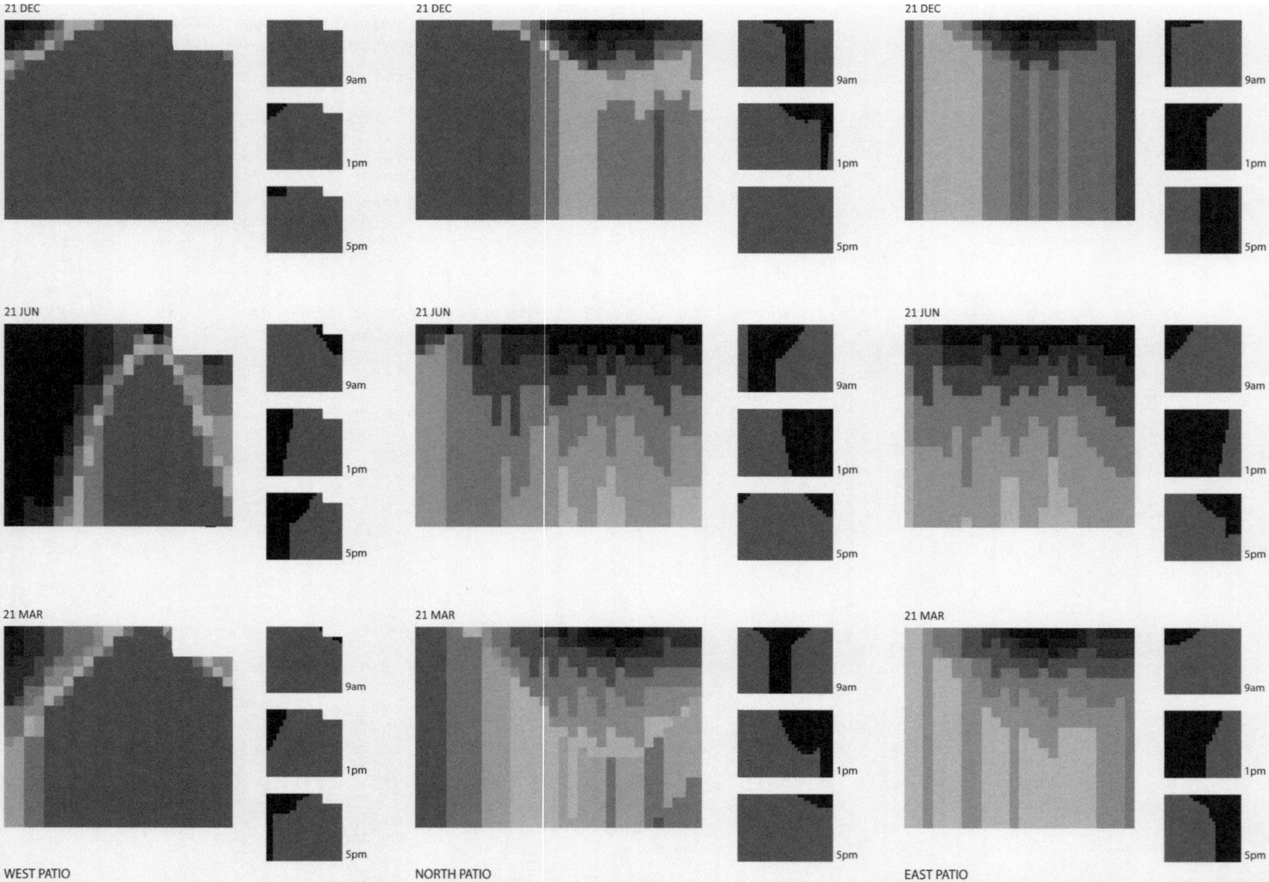

solstice was reiterated to compare and verify the results with the previous analogue method. Additionally, we also conducted a survey across key dates and times in a calendar year to determine the various depths of light penetration in each patio based on the sun's changing altitudes.

The maps of these two studies reveal clear moments of overlap from patio to patio, i.e., in the similar illuminated conditions read vertically across the three rows of the summer solstice analysis. This demonstrated their various degrees of complicity, sometimes in-phase and at other times out-of-phase, in generating a particular environment filtering inside the space of the house.

Fig. 85: Inverted corrugation creating deep shaded spaces into the mass of Column_4 of New Orders.

Fig. 86: In zones exposed to longer and greater sunlight, recessed channel spaces are dug deeper into the mass of the column, whereas in less exposed areas, they remain minimal.

Computational

Light is energy and not matter. It can be measured in terms of levels of intensity and amounts of energy it emits on objects at any given time. A third solar analysis addressed this, through a computational method of colour mapping the unfolded surfaces of each patio subjected to solar radiation across a calendar year. A similar empirical study was conducted during the prototyping of column_4 of New Orders. Feedbacks from solar exposure on the column's inner surface guided the undercutting of its thickness to create a series of shaded channels of varied deep spaces, on the inside. The principal objective remains the same as with the house patios: through solar analyses, to contextually project light onto the blank canvasses of the patio spaces, in order to render visible where to best integrate a further material accentuation, implemented at another operative scale.

Pleated Matter

The best identified areas for the material corrugations to take place were in active zones directly facing the openings of the living spaces and bedrooms located above. These direct axes to the concrete corrugations would create greater visual impact when seen from and through the interior space of the house. While the light shafts have identical dimensions in plan and elevation (4.5m diameter and 9m height), they have very distinctive characteristics, hypothetical to highly differentiated lighting qualities: they are oriented otherwise vis-à-vis the overall mass of the project and their environment. The north lightwell is fully enclosed in plan and only top lit while the east one is both top lit and open on its south side. The corrugation of the north patio would be oriented south-east and south-west for the east patio. These types of variables within variables are what give the house ultimately both its experiential unpredictability and subsequent spatial autonomy. It has a life of its own.

Fig. 87: Sun rising early morning in the northern patio; self-enclosed in plan, only top lit.

The main issue was to what degree and to what outcome a devised material accentuation, such as the concrete corrugation, which is inherent to an existing architectural element, such as the patio wall, can amplify the experience of its spatial and physical character.

Resource

The formwork material used for all the exposed concrete surfaces of the house employs pine timber boards that are 10cm wide and vertically oriented to create the various planar and rounded formwork enclosures. At the end, it was considered the most appropriate solution to construct the different size circular walls for patios, pool and bathrooms, at an acceptable level of resolution. The specified wooden planks became the scalar metric from which the geometry of the entire house was to be approximated. Since it included the cylindrical shape of the patios, it seemed sensitive for the desired corrugation to be generated by deviating some of the boards' original placements. One single geometrical plan specifying the boards' locations would suffice to define the corrugation and direct its construction, using the general contractor's own building techniques and material resources.

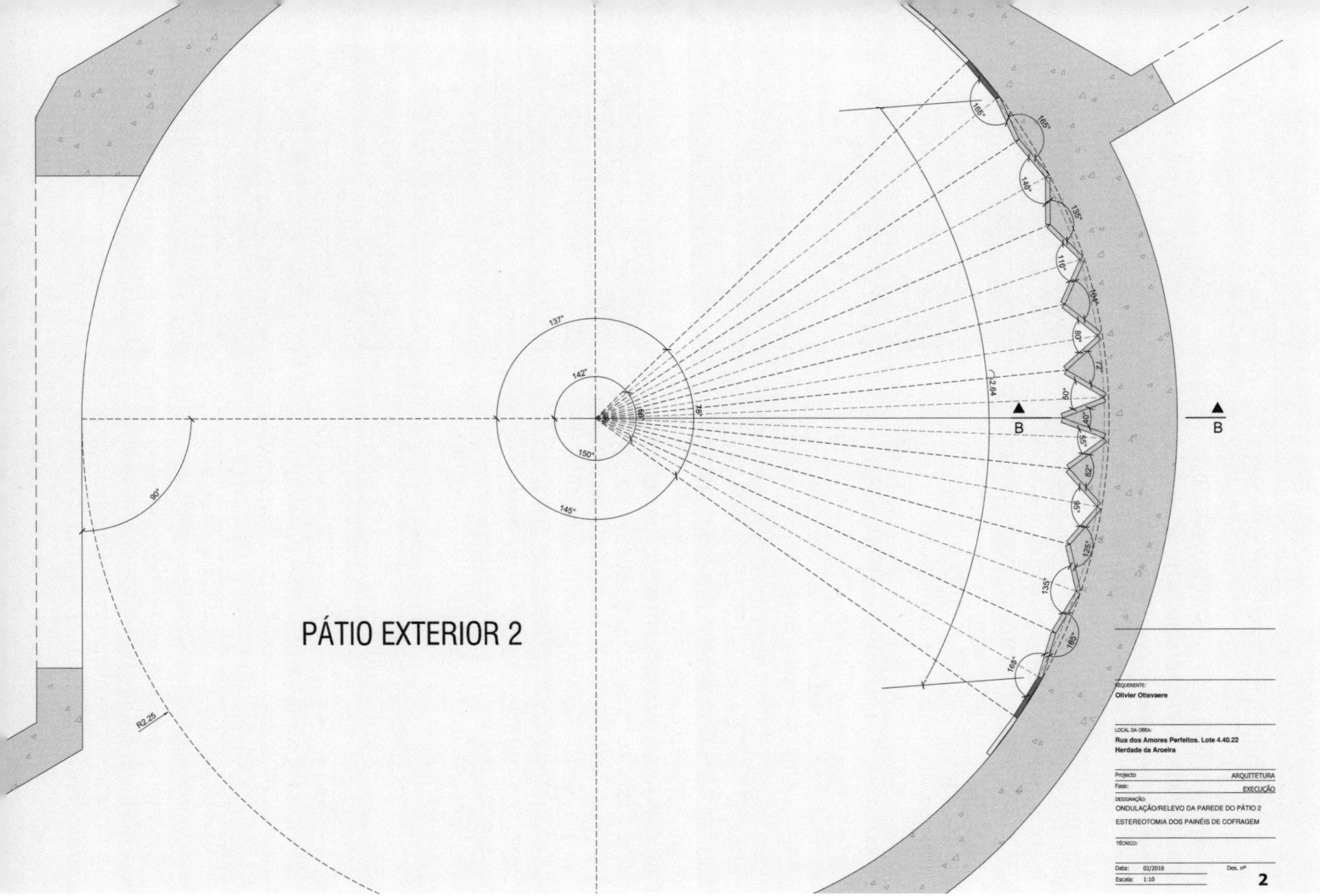

Fig. 88: Technical drawings of formwork geometry for the patios' corrugations: Horizontal section of the concrete wall, showing timber boards' layout in relation to concrete mass.

Technique

Following their initial cylindrical placements, the boards for the inner formwork of the patio begin to incrementally fold out of position, reaching their maximum crease at midpoint to then fold back progressively in their regular circular succession. Each corrugation was lifted 20 cm from the ground to produce an impression of lightness and to reaffirm its belonging to the vertical mass of the concrete wall. For the formwork construction, the corrugated geometry was directly translated into CNC-milled templates, assembled in a frame and onto which the timber planks were directly nailed into their exact positions.

Each fold used two 10cm-wide boards to retain a sense of size continuity with the rest of the regular patio wall. The same formwork was reused to make both patios' corrugations, as well as the three successive pours vertically, accounting for the 9m height of the walls. The process of formwork assembly and disassembly was cumbersome and time consuming. Like a piece of customised furniture, each formwork was manually reconstructed in-situ, board by board, in order to match timber traces of the previous concrete cast below. It was the only way to ensure vertical alignment of the boards' concrete texture from pour to pour. In doing so, it prevented horizontal misalignments which would have created visual breaks over the continuous vertical reading of the structure's massing.

Language

In concrete construction, form follows formwork reliably. The corrugation appears as if coming out of the mass of the wall itself upon some other kinds of external forces. Its incisive character increased by crisp yet open-ended shadow lines pushes away one's presence from the wall perimeter as if reminded that something else had taken hold of time. It displaces the subject from being at the centre of the experience. These crisp shadow lines present a sense of extended release.

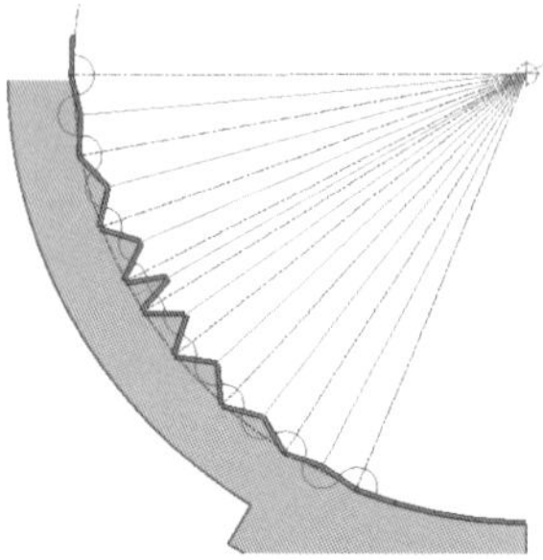

Fig. 89, 90: Concrete corrugation and its drawing specification for the making of the formwork: the boards fold incrementally to an acute angle of 40 degrees, then decrease back to their regular circular positions.

Fig. 91, 92: CNC-milled template for folded corrugation and their framework assembly to guide the placement of the vertical boards.

They are meant to accentuate the vertical reading of the shafts from below and exude a feeling of vertigo from above. When facing the patios from inside the house, especially mid-height at bedroom level, any references to ground and sky have disappeared. Only the evanescent light registered on the patios' corrugations shows any passage of time.

INSIDE-OUT
(on spatial responsiveness: interiority)

This last folio closes the sequence of nine in silence, at least where words are concerned. To measure some of the claims made above, a series of images were commissioned from an independent photographer whose brief was to survey the existential qualities of the house created by the sole participation of natural sunlight with material, structure, mass, scale and space. What follows is a series of test photographs, taken mid-construction, when the concrete body of the house was just completed and before the finishing phase of construction had begun. This brief moment of 'uncertainty' was captured while searching for the first time for ways in which pure structure could become absolute space and vice-versa.

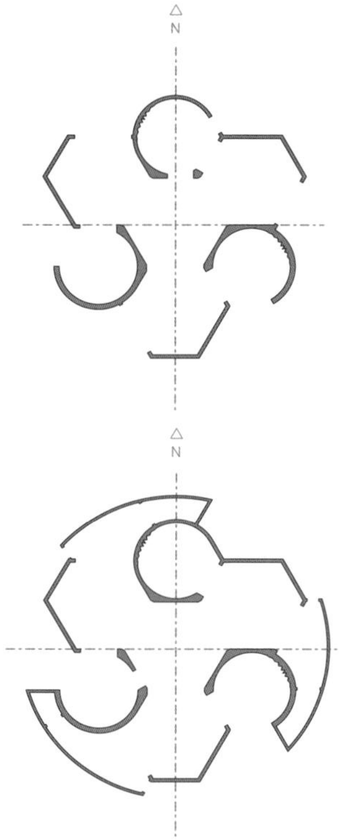

Fig. 93, 94: Ground and first floor plans showing the degree of porosity between inside and outside.

Fig. 95: Glass reflection through the space of the house: outside-inside-outside.

Fig. 96: Kitchen below and bedroom two above, with its ceiling plane cut through the swimming pool's underbelly.

97: View from bedroom one level, looking at bedroom two on the left bedroom three up on the right, with living room underneath it.

Fig. 98: Outdoor view into the east patio.

99: Semi-open east patio with floor-to-ceiling openings for
g room below and bedroom three above.

Fig. 100: Inside the space of the north patio.

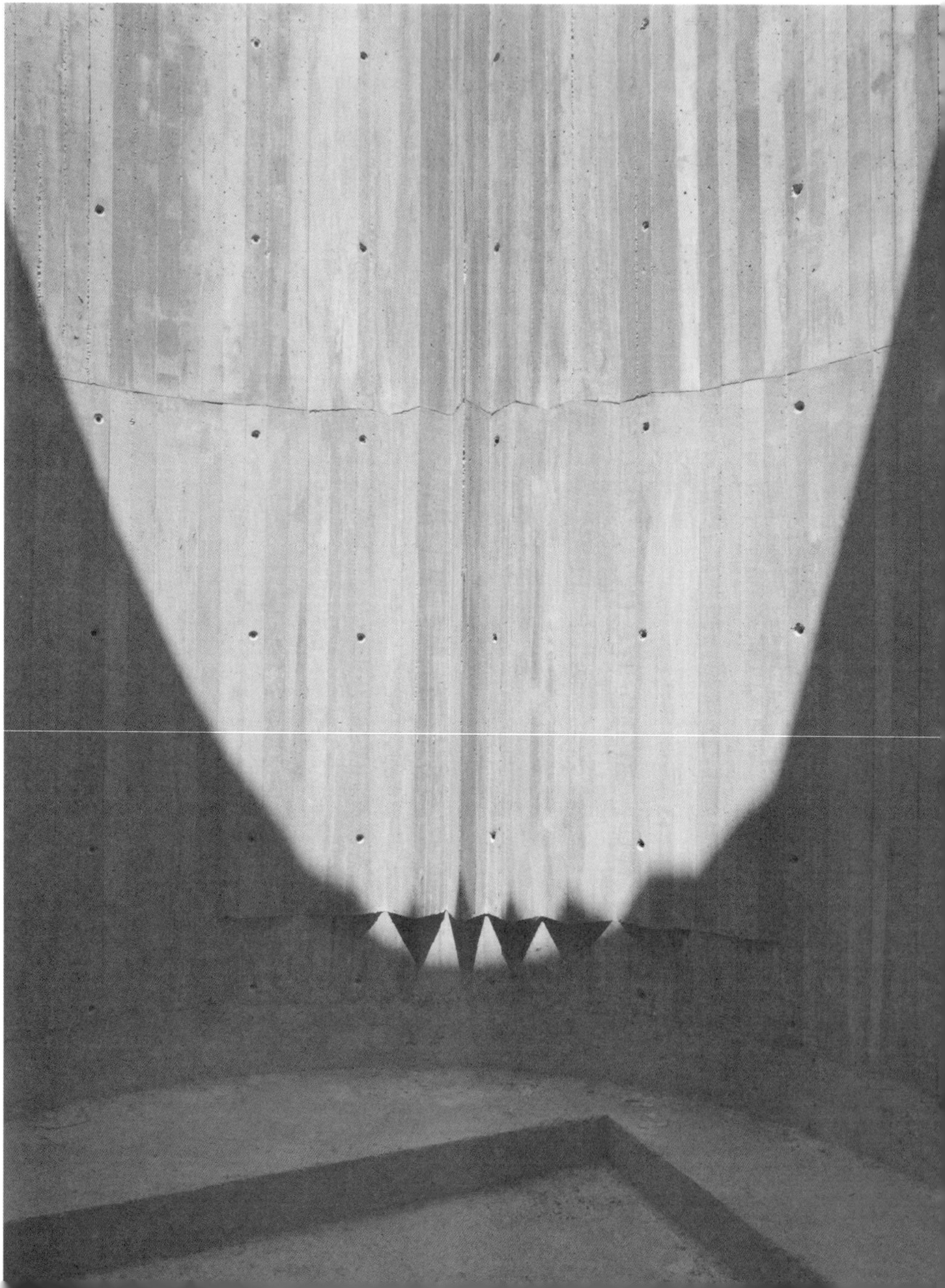

101: View of bedroom 2 with swimming pool volume above.

Fig. 102: Light from skylight entering bathroom.

103: Triangular skylight above atrium stairs, next to roof ace entrance via west patio.

Fig. 104: Light penetrating inside the north patio.

105: Looking through the kitchen space and into the north
y patio.

Fig. 106: West elevation looking into the kitchen space.

KEY DETAILS

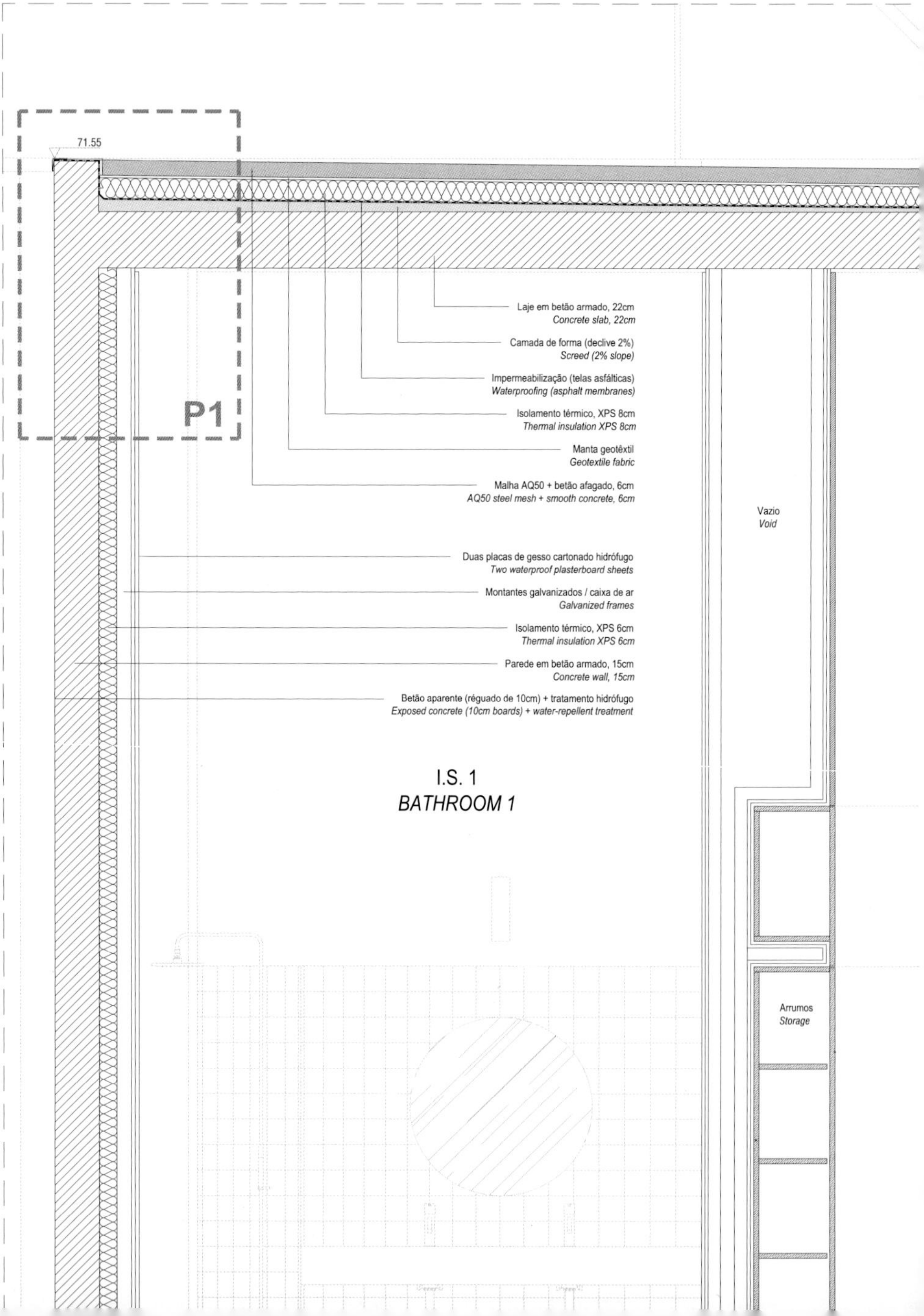
71.55
P1
Laje em betão armado, 22cm
Concrete slab, 22cm
Camada de forma (declive 2%)
Screed (2% slope)
Impermeabilização (telas asfálticas)
Waterproofing (asphalt membranes)
Isolamento térmico, XPS 8cm
Thermal insulation XPS 8cm
Manta geotêxtil
Geotextile fabric
Malha AQ50 + betão afagado, 6cm
AQ50 steel mesh + smooth concrete, 6cm
Vazio
Void
Duas placas de gesso cartonado hidrófugo
Two waterproof plasterboard sheets
Montantes galvanizados / caixa de ar
Galvanized frames
Isolamento térmico, XPS 6cm
Thermal insulation XPS 6cm
Parede em betão armado, 15cm
Concrete wall, 15cm
Betão aparente (réguado de 10cm) + tratamento hidrófugo
Exposed concrete (10cm boards) + water-repellent treatment
I.S. 1
BATHROOM 1
Arrumos
Storage

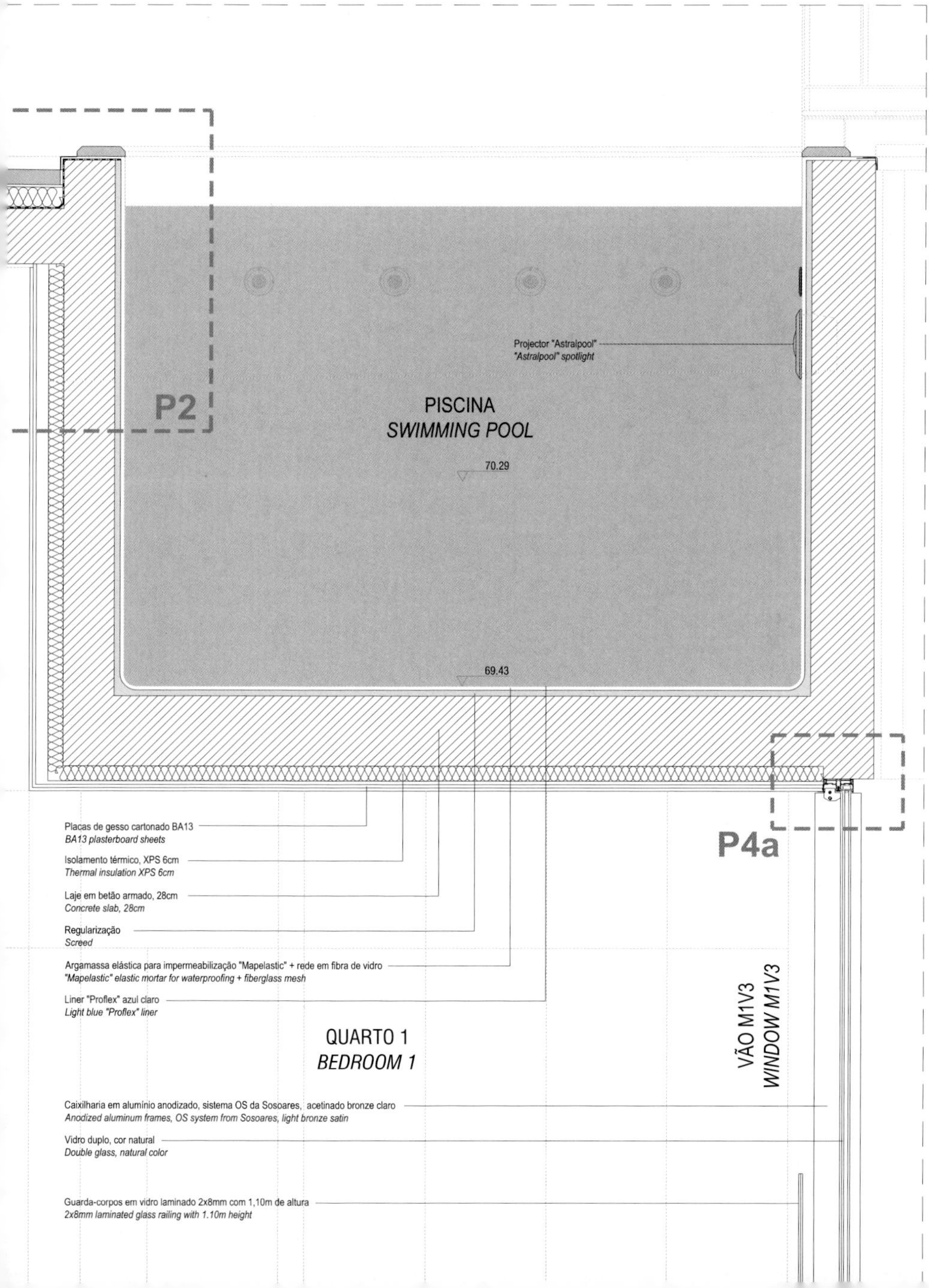
P2
Projector "Astralpool"
"Astralpool" spotlight
PISCINA
SWIMMING POOL
70.29
69.43
P4a
Placas de gesso cartonado BA13
BA13 plasterboard sheets
Isolamento térmico, XPS 6cm
Thermal insulation XPS 6cm
Laje em betão armado, 28cm
Concrete slab, 28cm
Regularização
Screed
Argamassa elástica para impermeabilização "Mapelastic" + rede em fibra de vidro
"Mapelastic" elastic mortar for waterproofing + fiberglass mesh
Liner "Proflex" azul claro
Light blue "Proflex" liner
QUARTO 1
BEDROOM 1
VÃO M1V3
WINDOW M1V3
Caixilharia em alumínio anodizado, sistema OS da Sosoares, acetinado bronze claro
Anodized aluminum frames, OS system from Sosoares, light bronze satin
Vidro duplo, cor natural
Double glass, natural color
Guarda-corpos em vidro laminado 2x8mm com 1,10m de altura
2x8mm laminated glass railing with 1.10m height

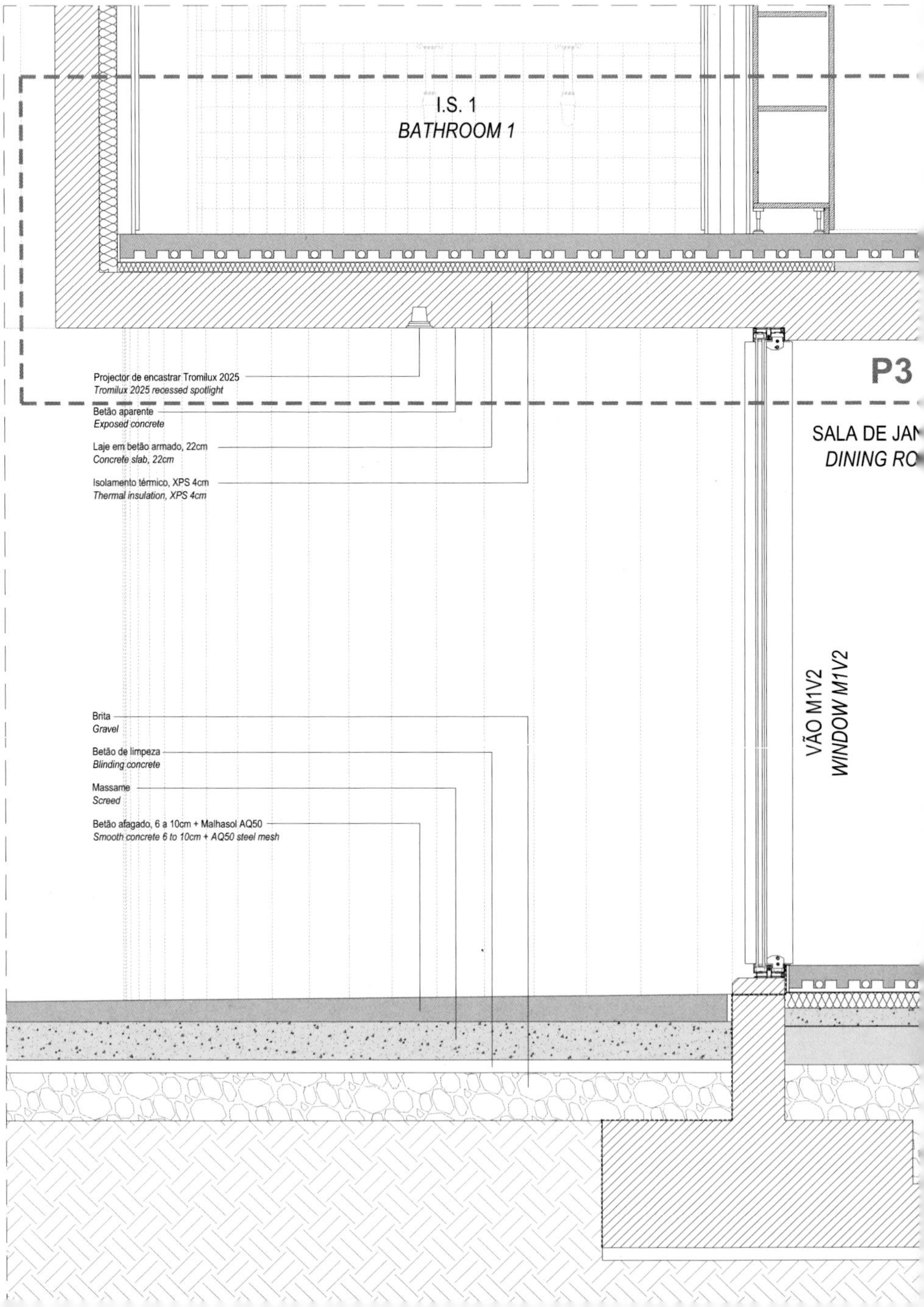
I.S. 1
BATHROOM 1
P3
SALA DE JAN
DINING RO
Projector de encastrar Tromilux 2025
Tromilux 2025 recessed spotlight
Betão aparente
Exposed concrete
Laje em betão armado, 22cm
Concrete slab, 22cm
Isolamento térmico, XPS 4cm
Thermal insulation, XPS 4cm
VÃO M1V2
WINDOW M1V2
Brita
Gravel
Betão de limpeza
Blinding concrete
Massame
Screed
Betão afagado, 6 a 10cm + Malhasol AQ50
Smooth concrete 6 to 10cm + AQ50 steel mesh

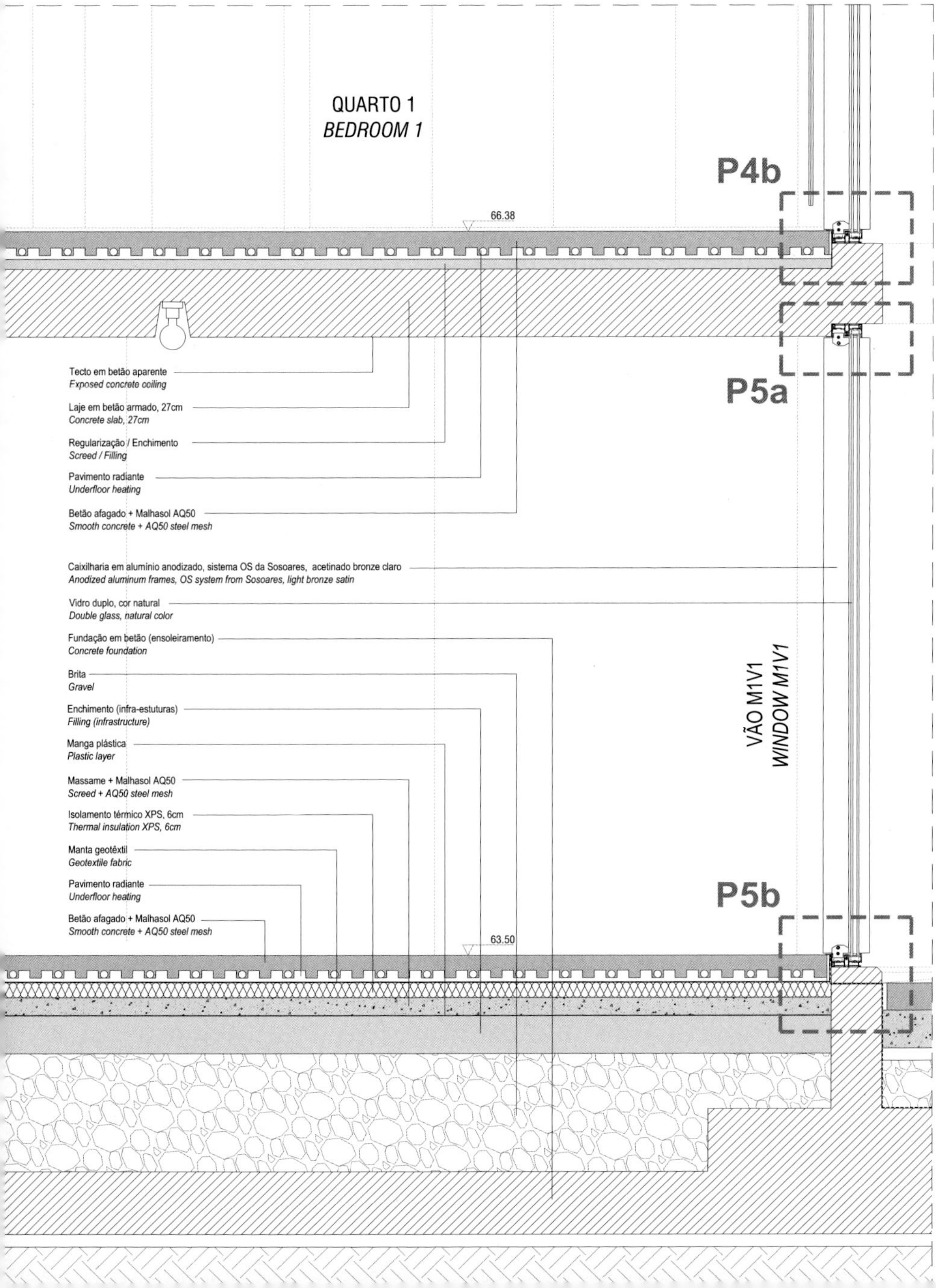
QUARTO 1
BEDROOM 1
P4b
66.38
P5a
Tecto em betão aparente
Exposed concrete ceiling
Laje em betão armado, 27cm
Concrete slab, 27cm
Regularização / Enchimento
Screed / Filling
Pavimento radiante
Underfloor heating
Betão afagado + Malhasol AQ50
Smooth concrete + AQ50 steel mesh
Caixilharia em alumínio anodizado, sistema OS da Sosoares, acetinado bronze claro
Anodized aluminum frames, OS system from Sosoares, light bronze satin
Vidro duplo, cor natural
Double glass, natural color
Fundação em betão (ensoleiramento)
Concrete foundation
Brita
Gravel
Enchimento (infra-estuturas)
Filling (infrastructure)
Manga plástica
Plastic layer
Massame + Malhasol AQ50
Screed + AQ50 steel mesh
Isolamento térmico XPS, 6cm
Thermal insulation XPS, 6cm
Manta geotêxtil
Geotextile fabric
Pavimento radiante
Underfloor heating
Betão afagado + Malhasol AQ50
Smooth concrete + AQ50 steel mesh
VÃO M1V1
WINDOW M1V1
P5b
63.50

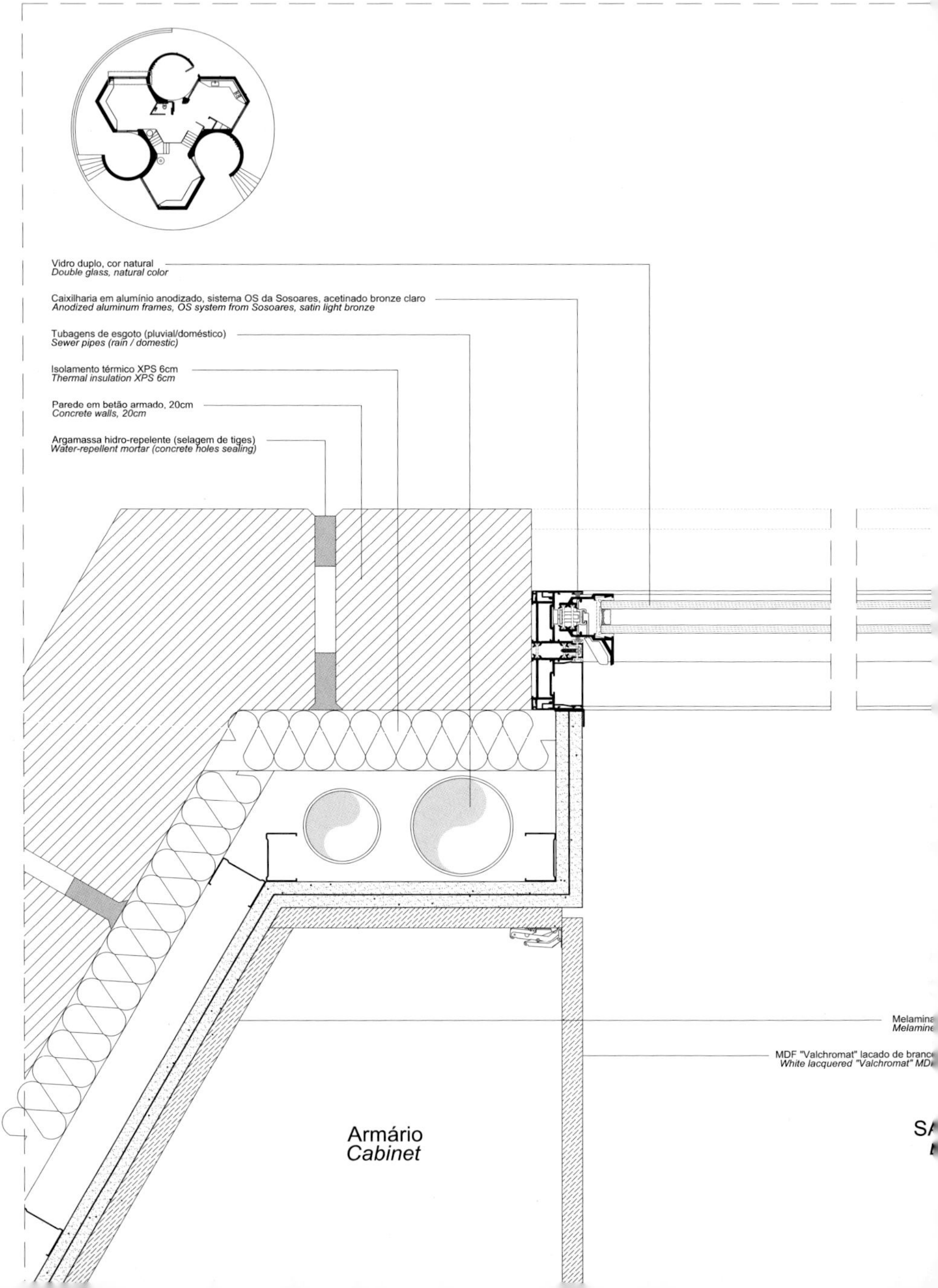
Vidro duplo, cor natural
Double glass, natural color
Caixilharia em alumínio anodizado, sistema OS da Sosoares, acetinado bronze claro
Anodized aluminum frames, OS system from Sosoares, satin light bronze
Tubagens de esgoto (pluvial/doméstico)
Sewer pipes (rain / domestic)
Isolamento térmico XPS 6cm
Thermal insulation XPS 6cm
Parede em betão armado, 20cm
Concrete walls, 20cm
Argamassa hidro-repelente (selagem de tiges)
Water-repellent mortar (concrete holes sealing)
Melamina
Melamine
MDF "Valchromat" lacado de branc
White lacquered "Valchromat" MD
Armário
Cabinet

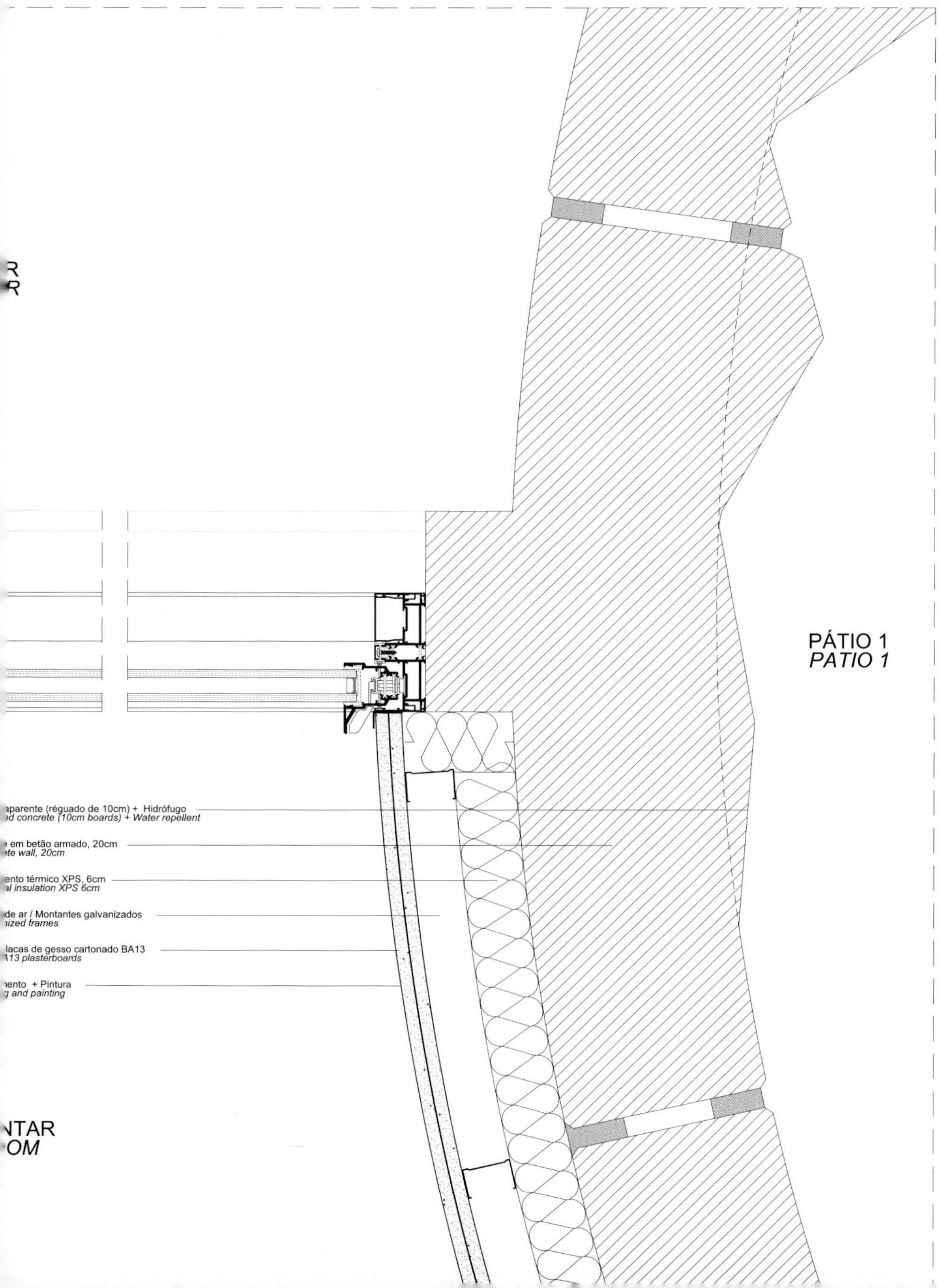
PÁTIO 1
PATIO 1
ıparente (réguado de 10cm) + Hidrófugo
ed concrete (10cm boards) + Water repellent
em betão armado, 20cm
te wall, 20cm
ento térmico XPS, 6cm
al insulation XPS 6cm
de ar / Montantes galvanizados
ized frames
lacas de gesso cartonado BA13
13 plasterboards
ıento + Pintura
and painting
NTAR
OM

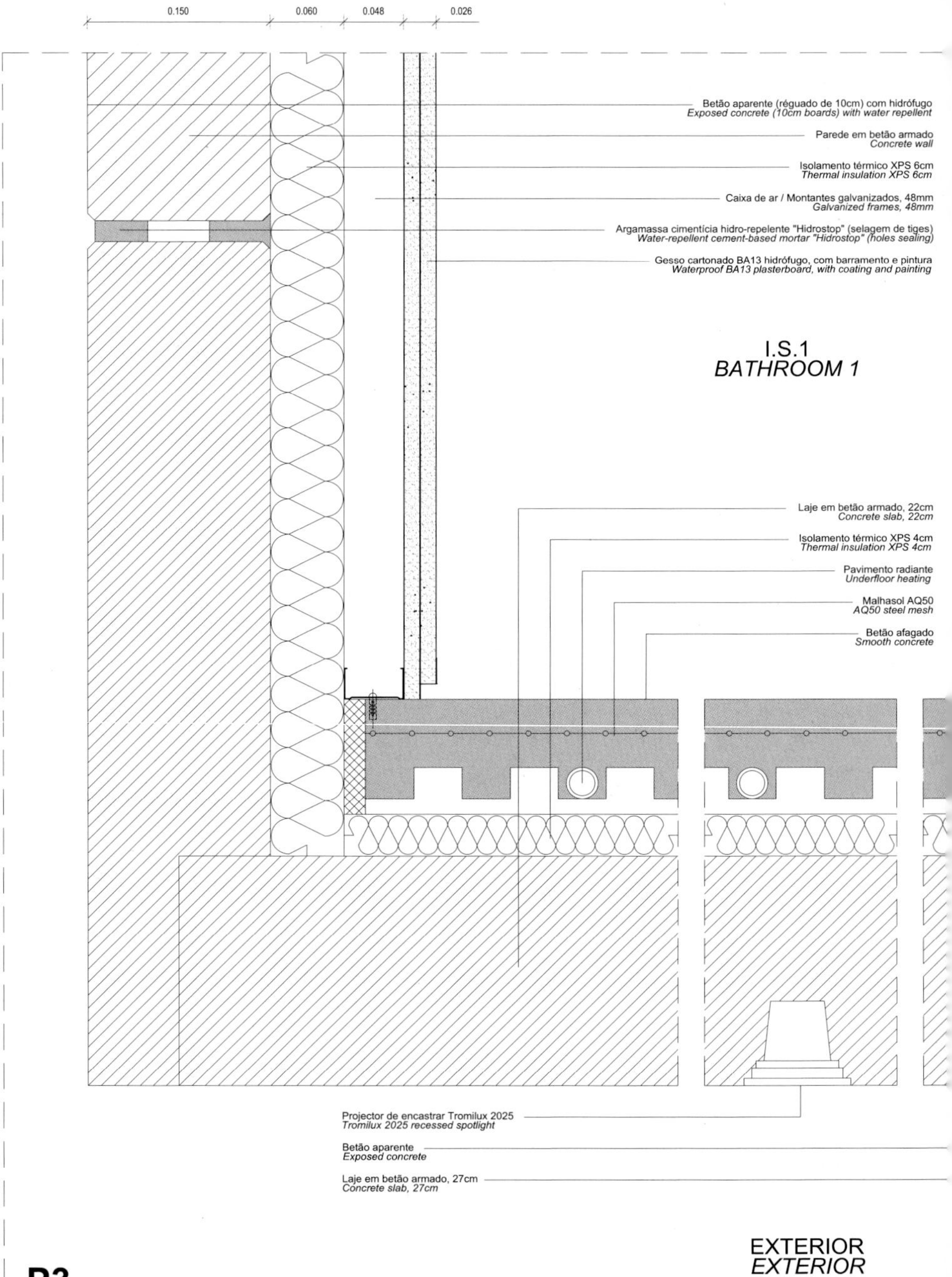
0.150
0.060
0.048
0.026
Betão aparente (réguado de 10cm) com hidrófugo
Exposed concrete (10cm boards) with water repellent
Parede em betão armado
Concrete wall
Isolamento térmico XPS 6cm
Thermal insulation XPS 6cm
Caixa de ar / Montantes galvanizados, 48mm
Galvanized frames, 48mm
Argamassa cimentícia hidro-repelente "Hidrostop" (selagem de tiges)
Water-repellent cement-based mortar "Hidrostop" (holes sealing)
Gesso cartonado BA13 hidrófugo, com barramento e pintura
Waterproof BA13 plasterboard, with coating and painting
I.S.1
BATHROOM 1
Laje em betão armado, 22cm
Concrete slab, 22cm
Isolamento térmico XPS 4cm
Thermal insulation XPS 4cm
Pavimento radiante
Underfloor heating
Malhasol AQ50
AQ50 steel mesh
Betão afagado
Smooth concrete
Projector de encastrar Tromilux 2025
Tromilux 2025 recessed spotlight
Betão aparente
Exposed concrete
Laje em betão armado, 27cm
Concrete slab, 27cm
EXTERIOR
EXTERIOR

P3

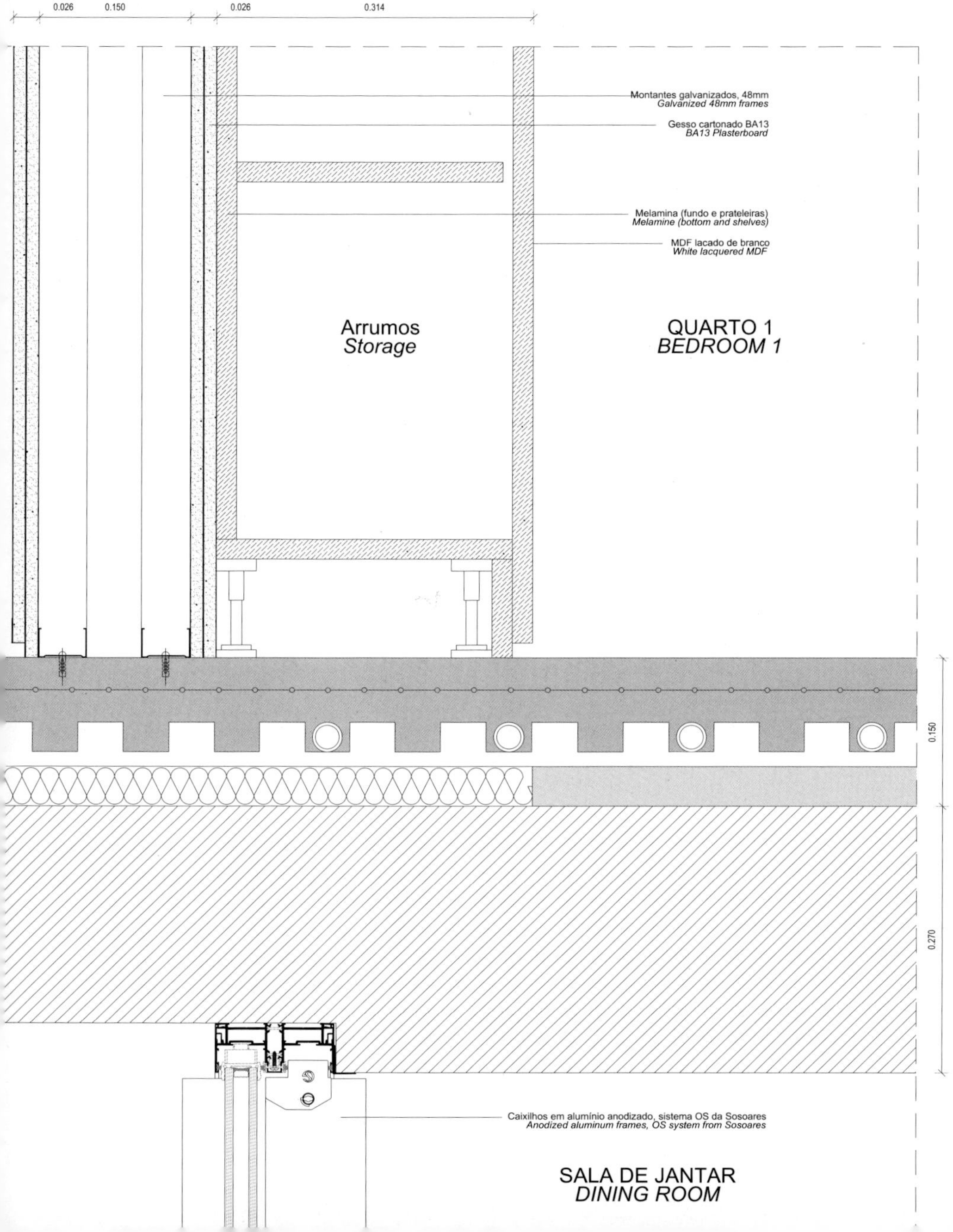

0.026
0.150
0.026
0.314
Montantes galvanizados, 48mm
Galvanized 48mm frames
Gesso cartonado BA13
BA13 Plasterboard
Melamina (fundo e prateleiras)
Melamine (bottom and shelves)
MDF lacado de branco
White lacquered MDF
Arrumos
Storage
QUARTO 1
BEDROOM 1
0.150
0.270
Caixilhos em alumínio anodizado, sistema OS da Sosoares
Anodized aluminum frames, OS system from Sosoares
SALA DE JANTAR
DINING ROOM

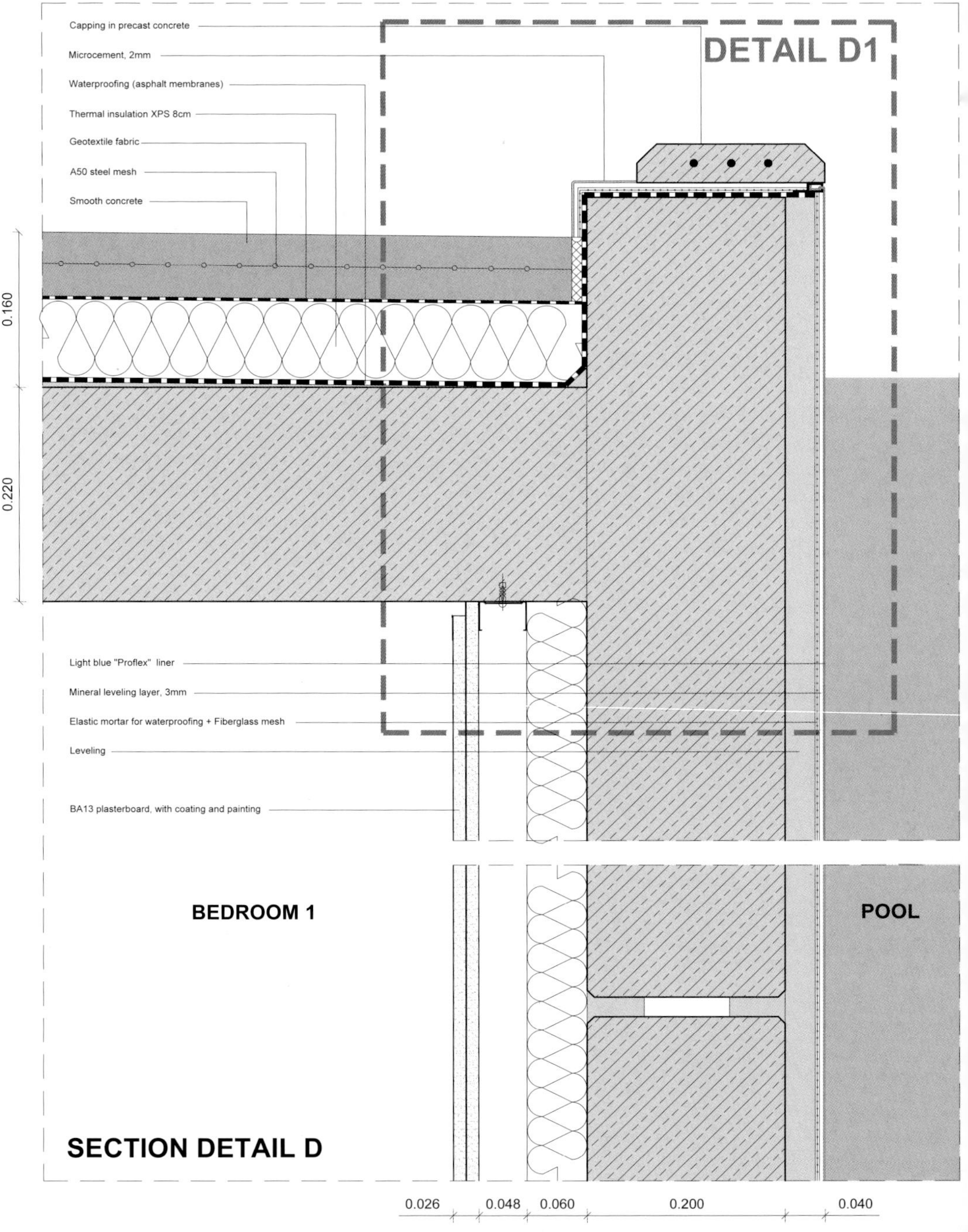

Capping in precast concrete
Microcement, 2mm
Waterproofing (asphalt membranes)
Thermal insulation XPS 8cm
Geotextile fabric
A50 steel mesh
Smooth concrete
DETAIL D1
0.160
0.220
Light blue "Proflex" liner
Mineral leveling layer, 3mm
Elastic mortar for waterproofing + Fiberglass mesh
Leveling
BA13 plasterboard, with coating and painting
BEDROOM 1
POOL
SECTION DETAIL D
0.026
0.048
0.060
0.200
0.040

THE BUILDING

PARTS UNSHOWN (CRITIQUE AND INTERVIEW)

PARTS UNSHOWN
BY DAVID ERDMAN

The experiential dimension of the late Anthony Bourdain's *Parts Unknown* TV series on CNN is an unmistakable hallmark of the show's long running success. Over five years, 12 seasons and 104 episodes, Bourdain eroded the boundaries between high and low culture, between the gastronomical and the ritual. His brilliance was finding what you could not see, what you could not taste, what you could not touch – while making you believe it was totally accessible. All that was required were the simple ingredients of equal parts of curiosity and open mindedness, intellectual fervor coupled with coolness. In his ongoing attempts to bring together things that often repel one another, Bourdain may have found his ultimate denouement, while spotlighting his generosity and beauty as a fellow traveller on the path of human life. From my perspective, he was a gifted architect and a kindred spirit of Olivier Ottevaere.

One might be struck, perhaps shocked, that an early career architect would work with concrete, the protagonist of unsustainable extractive construction practices driving climate change, in the twenty first century. It's still more unexpected to see them design a building with virtually no legible windows. Conjure a muted rock.

If we are to judge architecture on its appearance, Ottevaere's concrete absolutism, spanning from his experimental prototypes to Trefoil House, could be perceived as wildly anachronistic or out of touch with today's concerns and values. I would like to suggest otherwise along three axes of discussion.

Parts Unshown is an attempt to capture in a title, that among the objectives of the architecture Ottevaere has developed, is one that foregrounds the background. The design is attempting to presence what is not there. The continual positive-negative inversions, stemming from adroit methods of casting, give Ottevaere a unique combo of tacit material knowledge and a sensitive perceptual understanding of the shift of states between solids and voids. I would venture to say that his apparent objects are in fact in the service of their voids. The architecture's parts are what is unshown.

To this extent, the work bridges into profoundly contemporary territory. For centuries, architecture has been a game of addition and subtraction. While complex computational math has been thrown at it, architecture's 'mouthfeel' has limited complexity and has barely hit the level of basic three-dimensional trigonometry; in an experiential or dimensional sense. At best, architects activate the interstitial or the liminal: both of which suggest that the spaces between the parts (which are added together) are secondary, left over, on the periphery. Others have ventured to subtract from a solid, subjugating the void again to a second-class status.

Trefoil House is the culmination of multiple formats of casting and of varying densities of studying porosity. Ultimately, it flips an additive or subtractive ontology. The void comes first and the object second. It is designed for what is not seen. It is interspatial not interstitial. While the ingredients appear familiar – concrete, glass and void – the experience is wholly inverted.

Concrete Approximations suggests an oxymoron. In collecting a series of 'revolutionary objects', one might understand the work as closed figures, opaque, disconnected from their adjacencies. We could see this as an infatuation with concrete specifically. As a substance, as a material; this is a path well-trodden by architects that now lies before Ottevaere's generation of designers. I would suggest the 'approximations' we find throughout the book are to be found less in the literal unpredictable plastic material behavior of concrete than they are in their siting and contextual approach. For example, while Trefoil House has an apparent opacity, it is also highly centripetal, pulling the surroundings, their moods, their climates and their atmospheres into and through the building. What appears impenetrable is in fact effervescent, porous and deep. A measure of this effect is captured in TV shows like the Portuguese TV drama *O Clube*[1] who use the centripetal gravity of the project to great effect, weaving disconnected narratives, outsiders and residents into an intertwining of place and space, of crime and justice, of the formal and informal.

Details are often cited by architectural theorists, architectural historians and even by general enthusiasts as the ultimate test to determine the integrity of an architect; a measure of proficiency sometimes extended also to culinary artists and/or cinematographers. As an arrested fluid and a fairly crude material, concrete has seen many architects attempt to tame it, while others have celebrated its coarse, brutal roughness. Each opposing sensibility has a body of work and set of details associated with it; one might use either to try to measure the work throughout this book.

I would suggest something else is at play. Ottevaere seems to be toying with a different, less familiar and novel model of concrete 'detail.' The work collected throughout the preceding pages artificially inseminates concrete with ulterior motives, 'increasing' its potentials. Folding or creasing are typically strategies for sheet assemblies more than cast materials. Various scales of creasing in Trefoil House (in particular and perhaps more so than in earlier experiments) allow for folding and slicing to augment and animate the space, with and without humans moving through it. By creasing the architecture, Ottevaere's textural details enliven the environment, presencing it as another inhabitant of the space. He ritualizes the porous revolutions with rhythm, time, shadowplay.

Concrete Approximations is thus a book about what cannot be seen. It encapsulates a body of work spanning related prototypical projects, using

1 *O Clube* (The Club) - Série de TV da SIC OPTO (8 TV series episodes) where Casa Trevo was the house of the main protagonist and played a central role in the filming of the Portuguese TV series.

Trefoil House as its primary test case. Each test case and scale of work consistently foregrounds a provocative contradiction: that what is not shown (or seen) may be critical to the tacit and primal rituals of the architecture. Parts Unshown is perhaps best understood as a device to heighten our attentions, to make accessible what is unknown, allowing us to reconsider our habitats and how we might habituate space. The projects collected on the preceding pages embody the experience of revolving, exploratory, porous territories, even though they may appear to be a collection of singular concrete objects. They are approximate, secreted meditations in unleashing the dynamic potential of their 'unshown' parts.

INTERVIEW BY DAVID ERDMAN WITH OLIVIER OTTEVAERE

Objects For Voids

David Erdman: A quick read of the work might suggest an obsession with the opaque, the concrete. One could even misread it as objects in a landscape, but I think it is actually the opposite of that. It's in fact in the service of the voids. I'm interested in hearing more from you about this approach as a conceptual framework, methodology, and discourse, and its relationship to the work's legacy. We could talk about that first.

Olivier Ottevaere: When you first mentioned 'Objects for Voids', I actually thought you were spot on! I never thought about it this way. This was very unconscious from my side. At the time, I was experimenting a lot with small scale objects, concerned with concrete as a process. What interested me initially with working with concrete was not concrete per se (i.e., as a final material or its aesthetic aspects), but more about the procedure involved in working with concrete: it is multi-steps, multi-directional and as a consequence very undirect. Then, the obsession became about engaging actively with the properties of the concrete, such as liquid pressure. So, pressure, liquid and ultimately formwork design, the temporary part that is going to disappear, took hold of the prototyping method. By concentrating the attention on creating formwork, the articulation of voided spaces as positive volumes was prioritized over the gaps left in between them, where concrete would eventually be poured in. In other words, the making process, in forcing you to think negative (space), allowed the voids essentially to overcome the solids.

The house design though only came after this series of small casting experiments (i.e., the columns of New Orders). As a series, they were prompted by the transformation of precedents from 'structural mavericks', as I called them. These were people who in the past really pushed the limits of what could be done in concrete. Yet their progressive works were often singular in function and surface-like shells, horizontally articulated. With the columns, I transformed some of their projects' languages vertically in search of a new heterogenous architectural grammar.

Coming back to the voids' propositions in the house, they came directly from the translation of some of these self-made concrete precedents; the columns' prototypes. The voiding strategy in the house resulted in the intersection of previous ideas that operate at different scales simultaneously. For example, a search for permeability at the object scale (the entire house), mainly conceived in plan, at the tectonic scale; the idea of deep recessed spaces in the name of the three patios; and the concrete folding within the patio spaces, "Increasing" as you called it, at the detail scale.

DE: It is interesting. I now want to contemplate a little bit on the subject of 'Objects for Voids'.

On one hand there's nothing innovative about the casting technique. What I find relevant is the tacit knowledge that you gain from the many experiments you have done. It's not just about the geometry, but also about the shifts from solid to void and exploring the effects of pressure and other factors. This gives you a different ability to work with voids, as you are essentially making the voids as solids first. The rigorous experimentation and shifting geometries give you a good feel for this process, which is why I call it tacit knowledge.

When it comes to the Trefoil House, of course, you can't do everything yourself in a one-to-one manner. Some of the things you and other contractors made are literal indexes of the process itself, and while the Trefoil House has some of that, it is also an assembly.

In Kahn's work, there is a strong emphasis on volumetric form, an assembly of big volumes. Rudolph's interest lies in the voids, although they are considered secondary, appearing as cracks or interstitial spaces.

So, I wonder if you can just talk a little bit about that, in terms of what I referred to as 'Interspatial versus Interstitial'. Is that something you were aware of? That you have an enthusiasm about this as a discourse? Is there politics to that which you think might be important, that shifts your work beyond some of those canons? I have some ideas about that, but I'd be curious to see what you think.

Interspatial versus Interstitial

OO: In regards to the notion of the 'Interspatial versus interstitial', I still believe to this day that architecture is autonomous, that it exists before people. It is not meant to be anthropomorphic, at least as a pre-condition. In other words, there is more at stake than the subject being at the center of the experience.

To achieve this idea of the interspatial, many leakages were created in the geometry of the plans of the house, such as incomplete figures, absorption of circles and polygons that were left open in many directions.

The intention with the Trefoil, or three-partite structure, was to suppress any notions of symmetry or binary dialogues between architectural elements, rendering its reading more dynamic. Also, there are no right angles. That is to say, there are no stationary positions one can refer to or [where one can] pause for a moment.

Spatially, all the rooms are also unbounded. They fuse into one another. As a subject, you are always sandwiched between views, inside and outside of the house perimeter.

> It's centripetal as well as centrifugal. The house invites nature and light in, but it also leaks out into the context via large windows across rooms. Furthermore, it expands and contracts based on seasons (outdoor living in the summer versus more introverted living in the winter.
>
> The initial approach was to conceptualize the structure as habitable space, achieved by raising the ground to the roof datum. This led to the creation of patios or lightwells, which are essentially hollow columns that are semi-open, allowing the surrounding context to be invited in. Acting as three large jacks supporting a beam of water nine meters above ground, which weighs a substantial 100 tons. The house is then situated beneath and between these outdoor patio spaces. The rooms filter through these columns in an open and informal manner, causing the subject to never fully settle in.
>
> Furthermore, the natural light that penetrates these lightwells creates a constantly shifting and overlapping experience. The resulting space is very fugitive, evanescent and effervescent, as you mentioned in the preamble. This exemplifies the interspatial, where the space within the house exists beyond the subject's perception. The subject is merely a temporary witness of something larger that they can never fully comprehend. At best, one becomes a speculative participant in this experience.

DE: You're discussing another subject I want to talk about. It's a mistake to only understand the building in plan – the trefoil is actually made up of multiple incomplete figures, creating six to eight void objects when fused together. This adds complexity and exaggerates the qualities of agitation and dynamics. Rudolph's roughness is also dynamic, but it's through the assembly of concrete things rather than voids. His voids crack and leak, but they add up to something interesting because architecture historically prioritizes the module as the sealed weather environment and habitat. However, your approach puts pressure on the solid elements, emphasizing the medium of the voids, which pulls in other media and breaks the house open in a way that's more primary than Rudolph's interstitial approach.

This creates an interesting advocacy or equivocal hierarchy of the environment with the architecture. It's similar to Ryonaji, a Zen temple in Kyoto, which objectifies the void as something you can't go into. The void is not absence in Japanese philosophy, but something. The ritualization in your house is not dissimilar from Ryonaji's approach.

It's a different mathematical framework for understanding addition or subtraction, and I see it as a contextual approach. Your architecture is somewhat autonomous, but the voids also bring in the dynamics of the environment as a primary medium, making it a contextual approach.

> OO: Yes, the environment, especially Lisbon's brash sunlight, is the medium that animates the house in most unpredictable ways. More on that later. I wanted to go back to what you began with, in saying it would be a mistake trying to understand or make sense of the house in plan.
>
> The plan is just a base for a work in section to take place. I consciously made all the rooms the same shape, area and size as reference (starting point). But volumetrically they are all very different because all the ceiling heights change from room to room. Yes, if you read it in plan it looks fairly repetitive. But one would never experience that in reality since it is not how it works in section.
>
> If you take the bedrooms and ensuite bathrooms as example, the three of them are identical in plan yet in section the first one feels too large (5m high), the second just about right (3m) and the third almost too low (2m), and

this is further exacerbated by having the underbelly of the pool cutting through the ceiling of two of them, creating another height shift. I am interested in these changes and collusions of scales and in the feeling they give back by comparison.

In regards to voids as objects, I would like to point out that the most surprising and indeterminate void in the house is the central space; the Atrium. At the bottom, it is completely open, unbounded, it leaks into all the rooms, before it progressively solidifies as it rises up. It's nine meters high. It feels almost like a church or chamber-like space where all the design elements converge on its periphery, synthesizing the project's interiority. As one circulates towards the top of the house, it projects a unique spatial experience vertically.

DE: I found 'O Clube' revealing in the clips I watched. There is the spinning gravity in plan but there is also a sectional gravity because it compresses as it goes up, and that seems very intentionally used by the director as a device to bring together things that otherwise wouldn't be woven together. It is used as a narrative and plot device the way you were just describing it in section. It brings together outsiders and residents, the prostitutes and the clients, it brings together crime and Justice, the formal and informal spaces.

OO: It is interesting you mentioned that, because obviously I gave them carte blanche. It was done by a successful film director, Patricia Sequeira, and you're right, all the scenes are cutting the central space in a way that the atrium becomes the center of all the actions.

DE: Yes, she was able to understand it cinematically and really use the architecture as a great device, as a great narrative. I don't think you could do that in a different building that doesn't have those qualities. The way she shoots that is quite compelling and is a testament to the framework that you've thrown into it.

OO: Actually, I would like to bring back the idea of the revolution, the use of the circle as main figure and its associated zonal qualities as a device not to arrest or frame any privileged views.

Also, the intentional dichotomy between the interior and exterior. It was very important that on the exterior, the idea of the monolith was kept to avoid creating any breaks or visual interruptions that may reveal any clues about the interior arrangement.

I am mentioning this because in your preamble you stated, 'a house with no windows'. Actually, there are, and huge ones. They are simply not recognizable from the outside, which was a conscious choice as well.

DE: Of course, but people could read that as a house with no windows. What I said was with 'virtually no windows', virtually not like 'almost', but virtually like 'that's a virtual effect'. Yes, it seems like it has no windows but it actually has a lot of windows.

OO: I do get that question a lot, often by passers-by, 'Where are the windows?' It's a popular misperception of the house seen from the outside. Another conscious decision was not to leave any traces of the horizontal slabs shown on the outside periphery.

DE: Yes, so you can't tell where the floors are at all.

OO: You cannot. Also, verticality governs structurally: walls comes first and slabs second as a way to break the dominance of the horizontal datum into bits that could suddenly be placed at any desired heights.

The structure was done in three pouring cycles, which had nothing to do with where the different levels in the interior were located. In other words, it does not follow the conventional slab-wall-slab type of constructional hierarchy.

Projecting Nature

DE: Very unusual as you said, it's usually built in a very additive manner as opposed to a derivative manner.

I want to talk a little bit about the detail and the idea of creasing and folding, which is an interesting approach. As I point out in my text, that's an approach that historically and maybe unprecedentedly was never done in concrete; or at least in the manner you have deployed it.

> OO: While prototyping the columns, I was exploring a lot of these types of details, such as bulges, corrugations, crenelations, most of them emerging from the interaction of fabric formwork with concrete pressure. I call them material accentuations.
>
> As for the house, I really wanted to use the patios, that receive a particular kind of light and shadow cast, mainly elliptical, as a canvas for something else to be accentuated at another scale; hence the creation of concrete creases. Folding in and out of the thickness of the wall and hovering from the ground. they amplify the vertical reading of the patios while emitting a sense of vertigo. Inside the space, they project out at you, almost pushing you back. They give out something, creating an effect of awe.
>
> Materially, they were made using the same wooden planks to cast the house, ensuring a continuous integration with the rest of the concrete work. It does not read as an applied or added texture.
>
> They really augment this idea of autonomy and sense of time, because you become quite conscious that something is moving rapidly in front of you while not being able to see outside. Also, the light quality differs from patio to patio. They propose a very indirect presence of the environment, all animating the space of the house at different times.

DE: That's a beautiful way to ritualize the environment. It's that indirectness, that haptic sense of it evolving through the day while your day is progressing that makes it really give a presence. That is very different than if those were smooth voids, or, as you're saying, if they had an applied texture. The creases operate at a weird scale, a very awkward and effective scale, and they tinker in a subtle way with the fluctuations of the day through lighting. The creased baffles within the conically overlaid voids have some sonic effects as well?

> OO: There is also something else that is going on, that emerges as a surprise; this idea of suspension of time because a double shadow is being cast. The elliptical shadow of the object, the drum, overlapping with the shadows of these creases but out of sync, as if being delayed. That's why I call them light grinders.

DE: It's interesting because in academia, in popular culture and in various circles in the field of architecture, discussions about nature are often caricatures, in the worst case it's green bling. It's like, 'Oh, there's nature, we're going put a tree in it, it's natural.'

The philosopher John O'Donahue has an interesting book called *The Inner Landscape* focusing on aspects of perceptual beauty. He basically talks about nature as clocks that don't align with our circadian rhythm. He suggests the concept of God comes from the recognition of other clocks that we cannot make. That we innately understand things based on our own circadian rhythm and heartbeat, and so when you see things that are moving on very different clocks, they are intrinsic, like watching a river go by or watching the shadow play of leaves. If you really think about the beauty of nature, what you're watching are those effects that are not the tree per se. It's in fact how it's interacting with the environment – the rustling, the sound, all of those are all registering different rhythms that are made by things that we cannot make. This is what he is arguing. That it really produces a high degree of attentiveness and that's why I use the term ritualizing in my text very specifically because I think there is an aspect of this where you're capturing those clocks. As you're saying there are multiple shadows crossing over each other because of different and multiple shadow densities. All of that would be things that we would ambiently notice in the building without looking outside and without seeing a plan, we would be highly aware of something other in the house that is not us. There are no plants, it looks totally concrete, but you could argue that it has a highly natural set of effects.

> OO: Yes, there is only so much one can anticipate in terms of the design of it, of its interaction with the environment or the light. So many other aspects are completely unpredictable and came as a surprise. For example, the oscillating shadow of the surrounding pine trees caused by the nearby ocean breeze, being cast on the almost austere concrete surfaces and giving out this sense of softness in place of hardness. It feels very contradictory, almost like the subversion of nature registered onto the object.

DE: It makes it a kind of screen for the cinema of the surroundings that can be projected onto it. Yes, of course, you can't predict those things, and I think that Trefoil stages environmental effects. There is obviously a conscious – maybe slightly unconscious – understanding that you are putting something into play there that is going to interact with the surroundings in an intriguing way.

You may not know how that is going to play out, and there are likely to be some moments in your career, past and future, where it is not doing enough, but you seem to have found a pretty nice balance and, in this project, at least, you nailed it.

> OO: I like the synthesis of it all and how all the parts are coming together as one entity. For instance, yes there is a hierarchy of scales but each is not saturated, allowing them to

> interact with each other. All the design moves are also complementing one another, they are consequences to certain things happening for others to take over. Therefore, it is not additive in the way that this is where this thing takes place, and then next to it is this other thing that is occurring. Instead, it is very fluid, as in with the interaction with the environment.

DE: Thinking about more complicated hybrids and mixtures, you again use the void as a solid but the voids are not completely closed figures. They are doing different things. It is not additive and there is space in between.

Regardless, I love the idea that a house which presents itself as an object is in fact presencing the voids. This inversion is both brave, counter-intuitive and risks political anachrony. But I think much of that is avoided by placing the object in service of the voids, by giving presence to what is unshown. I cannot wait to spend some time in it!

PROJECT CREDITS

Project New Orders

Design:
Olivier Ottevaere,
Elsa Caetano

Project team:
Chong Chak Yuen Jason (project manager)
Kai-hong Chu Anthony
Chen Beining,
Ahn Byungchan BC
Au-Yeung Wing Man
Yuen Wai Yin Alex
Barrett Jordan
Zhu Jiqi
Justin Yeung

Project Casa Trevo

Architects:
Olivier Ottevaere
Elsa Caetano

Project team:
Hung Chi Lok Ernest
Kent Mundle
Chui Yvonne

Local architect:
Marco Antunes

Structural Engineer:
Joao Silva

Contractor:
CS Construtora

CONTRIBUTORS

Olivier Ottevaere

Is an architect and educator based in Hong Kong, China. He is the founder of Double(O) Studio and an associate professor in practice at the University of Hong Kong, China. His interest in architecture is driven by a hybrid approach between physical experiments and geometrical organizations. Integration of active structural principles, live properties of materials and inventive procedures of construction prompt the design pursue at the onset of each of his projects. Trefoil House in Lisbon, Portugal, as part of his broader practice-research work on prototyping with concrete, puts forward a built architecture where material, structure, mass, scale and space has become one entity inseparable from the user's experience.

David Erdman

Is the chairperson of Graduate Architecture and Urban Design and the director of the Center for Climate Adaptation at Pratt Institute in Brooklyn, NY. He was a co-founding partner of the design collaborative *servo* where he designed and completed numerous projects exhibited in museums in North America and Europe. Erdman co-founded *davidclovers* (now plusClover) with former partner Clover Lee where from 2006-2016 he designed and completed over twenty built projects in Hong Kong, China and North America.

In addition to the receipt of numerous awards and having work from both firms widely published, exhibited and collected in museums, Erdman was awarded the prestigious Rome Prize in 2008-2009.

Something Fantastic

Was founded by Elena Schütz, Julian Schubert, and Leonard Streich based on the conviction that architecture is related to everything and the resulting social, ecological and political responsibility demands a different practice. The work of the 'undisciplinary' office includes research and teaching in addition to the conception of books, exhibitions, furniture, buildings and urban planning. Having taught the MAS Urban Design at ETH Zurich, for several years the partners have now heading the Space Department at the Gerrit Rietveld Academie in Amsterdam; their current visiting professorship at the Peter Behrens School of Architecture Düsseldorf is entitled 'All-inclusive Urbanism'.

PHOTO CREDITS

pp. 106-17, and pp 130-49: © Fabio Cunha
pp. 46, 62, 63, and 70: © Marco Antunes

IMAGE COPYRIGHTS

Page 13

Fig. 3: Félix Candela Papers, C1455, Manuscripts Division, Department of Special Collections, Princeton University Library.
Fig. 4: Maison Dom-Ino, not located, Foundation Le Corbusier /ADAGP.
Fig. 5: NAM/SIAF Cité de l'architecture et du patrimoine/Archives d'architecture du XXe siècle.

COLOPHON

ORO Editions Publishers of Architecture, Art, and Design Gordon Goff: Publisher; oroeditions.com; info@oroeditions.com; Published by ORO Editions

Author: Olivier Ottevaere
Book Design: Something Fantastic Art Dept.
Project Manager: Jake Anderson
Color Separations and Printing: ORO Group Inc.

10 9 8 7 6 5 4 3 2 1 First Edition
ISBN: 978-1-957183-53-4

Printed in China

Typeset in Centennial and Acumin

AR+D Publishing makes a continuous effort to minimize the overall carbon footprint of its publications. As part of this goal, AR+D, in association with Global ReLeaf, arranges to plant trees to replace those used in the manufacturing of the paper produced for its books. Global ReLeaf is an international campaign run by American Forests, one of the world's oldest nonprofit conservation organizations. Global ReLeaf is American Forests' education and action program that helps individuals, organizations, agencies, and corporations improve the local and global environment by planting and caring for trees.